THE ANGER BUSTING WORKBOOK

Simple, Powerful Techniques for Managing Anger and Saving Relationships

James A. Baker

Foreword by
New York Times Bestselling Author
John Bradshaw

Copyright © 2005
by James A. Baker

All rights reserved.
No part of this book may be reproduced, stored in a retrieval system, or transmitted in any form or by any means, electronic, mechanical, photocopying, recording or otherwise, without the express written permission of the Author or Publisher, except for brief quotations in critical reviews. Inquiries should be addressed to Permissions, Bayou Publishing, 2524 Nottingham, Houston, TX 77005-1412. Ph: (713) 526-4558. E-mail: permissions@bayoupublishing.com.

This publication is designed to provide accurate and authoritative information in regard to the subject matter covered. It is sold with the understanding that the publisher is not engaged in rendering legal, accounting, psychotherapeutic or other professional service. If expert assistance is required, the services of a competent professional person should be sought. From a Declaration of Principles jointly adopted by a Committee of the American Bar Association and a Committee of Publishers.

Permission granted for use of cartoons:
© 1994. The New Yorker Collection Mort Gerberg from cartoonbank.com. All Rights Reserved.
© 2003-2005. Cartoon Stock, LLC. All Rights Reserved.
© The New Yorker Collection 1992 Bernard Schoenbaum from cartoonbank.com. All Rights Reserved.

Used and modified by permission. Leon Hale, Houston Chronicle, July, 2002. © 2002 Houston Chronicle Publishing Company Division, Hearst Newspapers Partnership, L.P. All Rights Reserved.

Permission generously granted to adapt core concepts from Newton Hightower's *Anger Busting 101: The New ABCs for Angry Men and the Women Who Love Them*. © (2002) Bayou Publishing (Houston, TX).

Cover Design: Kathi Dunn, *Dunn & Associates*
Back Cover Writing: Susan Kendrick, *Write to Your Market*
Editor: Roger Leslie, *Roger Leslie Writing*
Printer: *Bookmasters*

Printed in the United States of America
ISBN-13: 978-1-886298-19-4
ISBN-10: 1-886298-19-X
Library of Congress Control Number: 2005903932

Publisher's Cataloging-in-Publication
(Provided by Quality Books, Inc.)
Baker, James A.
   The anger busting workbook : simple, powerful techniques for managing anger and saving relationships / James A. Baker ; foreword, John Bradshaw.
   p. cm.
   Includes bibliographical references and index.
   LCCN: 2005903932
   ISBN-13: 978-1-886298-19-4
   1.Anger. 2. Men-Psychology. 3. Man-woman relationships. I. Title.
BF575.A5H54 2005   152.4'7'081
                          QB101-201216

Bayou Publishing
2524 Nottingham
Houston, TX 77005-1412
www.BayouPublishing.com
(713 526-4558

THE ANGER BUSTING WORKBOOK

Simple, Powerful Techniques for Managing Anger and Saving Relationships

James A. Baker

Bayou Publishing
Houston, TX

"I'm *very* angry. What do you suggest?"

What People Are Saying About this Book

"This workbook helps men change. Use it. It will work."

—BILL O'HANLON, author/co-author of 21 books
including **Thriving Through Crisis**

"The *Anger Busting Workbook* is for anyone approaching the boiling point. A fascinating bestseller. I feel like you've been peering over my shoulder."

—FRANK DOBISKY, CEO
Dobisky Associates, Media Relations for Higher Education

"Recommended for all mental health professionals. Break through the rigid blind spots of addiction to rage."

—MARIAN YEAGER, Ph.D.
Enete and Yeager Psychological Services, Inc.

"Too many self-help books are long on theory and short on practical, simple solutions. Jim Baker has put together real help and hope for people at the end of their rope."

—TIM SANDERS, Chief Solutions Officer of Yahoo
Bestselling Author of **Love Is the Killer App**

"Anger is a cruel and dangerous master. Jim Baker performs an important service by helping people overcome self-destructive anger."

—RAMSEY CLARK
Former U.S. Attorney General

"A much needed and practical tool for helping angry men. Women with rageful partners cannot do without this invaluable workbook."

—SAM J. BUSER, Ph.D.
Past-President, Texas Psychological Association

"Jim Baker's *The Anger Busting Workbook* is the perfect guide for saving raging relationships."

—ANN RICHARDS
Governor, State of Texas

"Anger Problem? If you find yourself in a hole stop digging and read this book"

—BOB BRADLEY
Author of **Living with Manic Depression**

"Extremely valuable for partners of angry men."

—HARVEY B. ARONSON, Ph.D., MSW
family therapist, trainer, author

"Full of specific suggestions, this down-to-earth approach can help you handle anger and conflict in all kinds of relationships."

—DANIEL SONKIN, Ph.D.
Author of **Learning to Live Without Violence A Handbook for Men**

"The principles and exercises in *The Anger Busting Workbook* offer clear, simple, common sense answers for anyone who is searching for help in their battle with anger addiction."

—JOHN BRADSHAW
Author of New York Times Bestselling **Healing the Shame that Binds You**

"This workbook is full of life-impacting tools. It should be required for all therapists who attempt to assuage anger and ameliorate interpersonal relationships."

—HARVEY ROSENSTOCK, M.D., F.A.C.P., *Clinical Assoc. Prof. of Psychiatry & Beh. Sciences, Univ. of Texas Med. School, Houston, TX, Co-author,* **Journey Through Divorce**

Contents

Foreword 11
A Note to the Reader 13
Preface — Face Your Anger 15
Introduction 21
Part I — A Recovery Plan for Angry Men 31
    1   *Putting on the Brakes* 33
    2   *A Check-Up from the Neck-Up* 71
    3   *Put a Sock In It (Really!)* 99
Part II — A New Strategy for the Women Coping
    with Angry Men 127
    4   *Facing Facts: Unhappily Ever After?* 129
    5   *The Line in the Sand* 153
    6   *ABCs for Your Own Recovery* 179
Epilogue 197
Appendix — Leading Involuntary Anger
    Management Groups 199
Notes 207
References and Reading List 209
Index 211
About the Author 213
Ordering Information 215

To my family

Foreword

In all my years of helping addicts and their families learn to face the ravages of addiction and overcome it, I have never found an addiction that was easy to conquer. The power of shame is so relentless and its grip is very strong. For that reason, I am always overjoyed when a new tool appears that can help addicts get traction in the fight to take back their lives.

I want to congratulate my dear friend, Jim Baker, for bringing to us just such a tool. The principles and exercises in the *Anger Busting Workbook* offer clear, simple, common sense answers for anyone who is searching for help in their battle with anger addiction. Over the years, Jim has helped tens of thousands of people become successful in business through his powerful training techniques. It is exciting to me to see him bring that same expertise to the war on addictions.

If you are an anger addict, or in a relationship with an anger addict, this workbook is going to help you make sense out of the mess your life is in. Here you will find a road map to guide you, insights to encourage you, and practical, hands-on exercises to help you tell the truth to yourself as you plan your strategy for conquering anger. It is still up to you to do the work, and the challenge you face is a tough one. But if you are tired of the old excuses and the old results, you will find plenty of reasons to hope as you work through these pages.

Can a workbook change your life? Well, it depends. We could just as easily ask, "Can a canoe paddle change your life?" They are both just tools. But they can come in real handy if you are tired of staying where you are and you are ready to move on in your life. If you pick up either one and *really use it*, it might just lead to a "moving" experience. Good luck on your journey.

John Bradshaw
Houston, Texas

A Note to the Reader

Newton Hightower has been a good friend of mine for many years. I have a tremendous appreciation for the work he does and the program he has developed to help anger addicts achieve true freedom from a disease that causes such suffering to both them and the ones who love them. And I have been truly thrilled with the success of *Anger Busting 101: New ABCs for Angry Men and the Women Who Love Them*, the book that first presented Newton's program to the general public. Almost from the very beginning, Newton and I saw the need for a companion workbook to his award-winning book—something that would make the principles of his program even more useful and accessible to the people who need them the most. I was pleased and flattered when he eventually asked me if I could help bring this next phase of the dream into reality.

I don't know anyone who doesn't struggle with anger every once in a while. After all, anger is a normal emotion and most of us experience it in appropriate ways at appropriate times. However, for a certain portion of the population, anger is not just an occasional emotion, it is a way of life. They are gripped by rage in ways that tear apart the fabric of their relationships and create confusion and chaos in every area of their lives.

If you are such a person, or if you are in a relationship to someone who struggles with anger on this level, then please pick up this book and read it! Devour it from cover to cover; let these principles and exercises soak into your heart and become the foundation for a new way of thinking, acting and choosing. This workbook is designed to help you apply Newton Hightower's ideas in a step-by-step fashion, whether you are involved in therapy or not, whether you're thinking about entering counseling or have just finished counseling, whether you're using medication or not. I have observed Newton as he works with rageaholics, teaching them to apply these principles in their lives. I can vouch for the fact that this stuff really works! *It won't just help you change, it will help you change now*!

I count it a privilege and an honor to have had a part in making this life-changing material available to you—to anyone who is ready to be free from the cycle of rage and brokenness that is anger addiction. I extend to you my prayers and best wishes as you begin your journey toward wholeness. Please remember, if you don't quit, you can't lose.

Jim Baker

Preface

Face Your Anger

Yeah, we know. You don't have an anger problem. You are just surrounded by idiots and incompetents. Your kids are lazy and disrespectful; your wife is constantly whining and complaining about something; your boss couldn't manage his way out of a paper bag; and the freeway is a parking lot for morons. Nobody appreciates how hard you work or how brilliant you are. Talent like yours is going to waste in a shop full of zombies. You work hard all the time and some days you just get sick and tired of putting up with people who seem to enjoy nothing quite so much as pushing your buttons so they can make your life miserable. Anger? Man, they have no *idea* what it would be like if you ever *really* got angry. Just once, it would be nice if they would just shut their yaps and let you have some peace and quiet. But no! It is always **something**! You don't have an anger problem, you have a people problem. *People just won't leave you alone!* You don't want to get angry, but they just don't give you any choice. Yeah, we know.

Here is something else we know. You probably actually believe all the lies you tell yourself and all the smoke you blow at other people. We have met a thousand guys like you. They all tell different stories but they all live in the same houseboat in the same river called "De-*Nial*." You have been making excuses for the outrageous ways that you treat other people for so long that it is beginning to seem normal to you. You have been blaming other people for your raging, irresponsible attitudes for so long that you actually believe it is okay to traumatize and intimidate the people you love because it makes you feel like you are in control, at least for a little while. The technical term for this—the play on words we used above—is *denial*. It is a trick that people play on themselves when the truth is just too hard to face. So, you just pretend that it didn't happen, at least not the way other people say it did. Or you pretend that it wasn't as bad as other people say it was (another trick called minimizing).

But here is a term that might make better sense to you—brainwashing. You have been lying to yourself—brainwashing yourself—for so long that you programmed yourself into really believing that your anger is not really about you, it is about *everybody* else. You tell yourself that other people pushed your buttons, that they somehow triggered you or shoved you over the edge; you make it sound as if you didn't really have a choice. But you

did. And for a long time you have been choosing to hurt people with your anger, hoping it would make you feel better. And now you actually **believe it**. You won't even let yourself look at the truth anymore.

Take at look at this image on the left.

This little diagram is called the Johari Window—developed in the 1950s by a couple of psychologists named Joe Luft and Harry Ingham. It is called a window because, obviously, it looks like a windowpane, but also because it helps us to "look in" on the way relationships work. The diagram helps to describe the way personal information is shared or understood between people. The *top left* pane tells us that I reveal certain information about myself to everyone. The *bottom left* pane indicates that there is some information about me that I hide from just about everyone. The *bottom right* pane shows that there is some information about myself that I don't even understand, and nobody else does either. And the *top right* pane reveals that there is information about me that practically everyone else around me can and does know, but I don't. This is called a *blind spot*. We all have them. And what we can't see really can hurt us.

The Johari Window is an interesting tool that can be used to help individuals and groups work on many different communication problems, but for our purposes we are going to stay focused on the top right panel—the blind spot. As we have already mentioned, there are just certain things about ourselves that we don't see, and even if we could, we wouldn't see them or understand them the way those around us do. It is just human nature to either ignore, excuse or reinterpret our actions in a way that puts us in the best possible light. People with anger problems—we call them anger addicts—usually have huge blind spots where anger is concerned. Other people say we are shouting, when we think we are only trying to make a point. Others say we get too physical, when all we are trying to do is keep them in the room so we can talk through a misunderstanding until it is settled. Others say that we lose control when we get angry, when we are certain that we are only being firm, but reasonable. How can so many people get things so confused?

I know how you feel. It even happened to me, the author. I'll never forget the day that my wife, Pamela, told me that she could always tell when I was getting angry because I started using profanity. I was absolutely dumbfounded! (And a little bit insulted). I have always prided myself on being a reasonable guy who kept things under control. It took a lot—I thought—to get a real rise out of me. Why would she accuse me of something like that, when I knew that I was the picture of composure under pressure? It turns out that the reason she could accuse me of it was because it was true! Over the next several weeks I made it a point to be more aware of my behavior under pressure, and suddenly, there it was! I began to catch myself automatically, almost unconsciously beginning to let fly with a few choice words. This is called "anger seepage." Turns out that I am one of those guys who likes to keep things under control most of the time, but as that pressure starts to build it begins to leak out in subtle, sneaky ways. I had convinced myself I had it all together, but I didn't. My wife wasn't fooled for a minute. She could read me like a book where all I could see was blank pages.

The point of all this is that, as an anger addict, you have a ***huge blind spot*** where anger is concerned. First, you deny that you even get angry; then, when your anger gets so out of control that it is obvious to everyone including you, you deny it is your fault, instead blaming someone else for causing the problem.

This last trick—blaming someone else for *your* out-of-control anger—is an old dodge called "scapegoating." Most anger addicts are really good at this. I bet you know the drill. You and your wife get in a huge fight. You call her a bunch of really nasty names, at the top of your lungs. Then you pin her against the wall when she tries to leave the room. When she twists and shoves, trying to get loose, well, that really makes you mad. So you slap her across the mouth and throw her down on the floor. You would kick her, too, except that she rolls over and slides out the door before you can catch her.

And all the time you are telling yourself it is *her fault*; she deserves whatever she gets. You make her the scapegoat who gets all the blame for your mistakes. You tell yourself, if she hadn't spent so much money on clothes for the kids, you wouldn't have bounced that check. And if she would have just listened to you instead of mouthing off while you were trying to straighten her out about it, you wouldn't have called her all of those names. And if she hadn't tried to run away from you while you were talking to her, you wouldn't have had to grab her. And if she hadn't shoved you, you wouldn't have had to hit her. So the fact that she now has a black eye, a cut lip, a sprained shoulder and a knot the size of a walnut on the back of her head is because *she spent too much money on school clothes*! Are you kidding me? Or are you kidding yourself? You have just waded out into the middle of the De-Nial River up to your eyebrows, practically drowning in your own excuses. And ***everybody*** knows it, except for you!

And then, to make matters even worse, when it's all over and the damage has been done, you try to pretend that it wasn't that big a deal in the first place. "What is everyone staring at, we just had a fight, that's all! Can't people have a disagreement every once in a while without you people making a federal case out of it?" Sound familiar?

Look, everyone around you is staring because they are emotionally battered and bleeding. They saw what happened, they experienced the full force of your rage, and they can see you for what you really are—an out-of-control anger addict who refuses to take responsibility for his own actions. But you avoid facing your problem. That blind spot is trying to protect you from yourself.

Are You Ready to Look in the Mirror?

The Blind Spot is there for a reason. If you ever took a long, hard look at yourself in the mirror you might be shocked at what you saw staring back at you. It is too ugly and too embarrassing; perhaps it's better to just keep your eyes closed and hope nobody notices. Oops! Too late for that, I bet. Aren't you reading this book right now because your wife has told you to change *now* or she is going to leave you? Maybe you are reading this book because a judge has ordered you into anger management training or go to jail, or never get unsupervised visitation to see your kids again. Yeah, the secret's out. You might as well suck it up, take a deep breath, and get eye-ball to eye-ball with the man in the mirror. At this point he is your worst nightmare. He is also your only hope.

Go ahead; take a look. What do you really see?

Let's just say it in plain English—the guy staring back at you from that mirror is nothing more than an **old-fashioned Bully**. A bully is someone who keeps doing or saying certain things in order to have power over another person. A bully creates an atmosphere of fear, intimidation and anxiety—usually through outbursts of rage, name-calling, criticism, cruel humor and unpleasant physical contact—to break down another person's ability to stop him from getting what he wants. Bullies are selfish and self-centered on the outside, but usually very insecure and afraid on the inside. The fearful and insecure part of a bully would qualify for the lower right hand pane in the Johari Window, because it is not clearly known by either the bully or anyone around him. But, take my word for it; it is definitely true. Bullies keep on pushing and shoving and yelling and attacking and throwing their weight around because it is the only way they can think of to keep a tight rein on the people around them that they truly *need in their lives in order to survive*. Here's the truth: You are not really a tough guy at all. You are weak and afraid; you just don't want anyone to know it.

There are a lot of reasons that guys become bullies. We are not going to discuss any of them here because frankly, it doesn't matter. You can spend three years in therapy figuring out that part if you want to. The important thing is that it has to stop *now*. And it can. Quit making excuses. Get your houseboat out of "De-Nial." Face the man in the mirror. And get ready to change.

"And just who the hell are you to tell _me_ I'm entitled to my opinion?"

Introduction

You can change right now.

Pause for a moment and let those words sink in.

If you are holding this book in your hands, it is almost certainly because someone in your life—your wife, your kids, your therapist, your boss or perhaps a judge—has made it abundantly clear to you that you have to do something about your outbursts of rage, and you have to do it *now*!

Of course, this is not news to you; most likely, people have been telling you this for years. However, up to this very moment, you have been willing to settle for other options. For a while you could smooth things over by just apologizing and promising it would never happen again, and then sweeten the deal with flowers and a night on the town, or a new dress or, if your behavior was especially dreadful, maybe a cruise or a new car! But you can only make and break so many promises before people begin to suspect that you are just playing them; eventually, the stakes get higher and the pressure to actually change gets heavier.

Finally, you probably even agreed to get counseling, where usually one of two things happens. Very often, after about three sessions, you and your wife are yelling at each other even more because now she expects you to suddenly be Mr. Charming and see things her way all the time; nobody even gives you credit for showing up at these annoying sessions in the first place. You are very relieved when your wife, and the counselor, decide you shouldn't come back. On the other hand, sometimes counseling isn't so bad, especially if you get one of those "nice" therapists who lets you talk about what a terrible life you had growing up; one who seems to agree with you that your boss is completely unreasonable, your kids are ungrateful and your wife doesn't appreciate everything you go through to take care of everyone. Talking to this kind of therapist isn't so bad. Maybe you even start to feel safe and open up a little bit. You get in touch with some of your emotions and decide to work harder at doing better. Which would be great if you could live your whole life at the therapist's office, but eventually you have to go home. Once you get back on the highway with those stupid, idiotic drivers and fight your way back home to a house full of unreasonable, ungrateful people it doesn't take long for all those feelings of good will to erupt into another angry outburst. Your wife says she doesn't believe you are even going to counseling. Now, that hurts.

Of course you feel bad about those outbursts most of the time; maybe you even feel guilty. After all, you don't get up in the morning intending to punch a hole in the wall or call your daughter all those awful names or shove your wife into the coffee table. Deep down, you *know* that you are not that kind of a guy. People just don't understand you; they don't listen to you; they don't give you the space you need or the credit you deserve. Why are they always arguing with you and trying to get you to change? Why do they make your life so hard, especially since you are trying to do the best you can? It seems so unfair. And, anyhow, most of the time you had really good excuses for blowing up. Why don't those kids ever pick up their toys? Why do we always end up having corny dogs and tater tots on Thursday nights? Why does her family always want to plan stuff on the weekends? People are always blaming stuff on you when you are hardly ever the one who starts it!

So now it comes down to this. She says things have to change **now** or she is going to go on with the divorce. To make matters worse, the judge says that if you want to see your kids without supervised visitation, you have to do something about your anger immediately. Of course, this has made you pretty much a wreck at work, but no one wants to cut you any slack. They are giving you a wide berth and encouraging you to get some help. How could it have come to this? Your first marriage was bad, but you thought it was just because you were both too young. You really don't want to lose another relationship, but everything you do just seems to make matters worse. What next?

The More You Do What You Always Did, the More You Will Get What You Always Got

Y*ou can change right now*. This isn't an empty promise or a therapist trick to get you to commit two more years and thousands of extra dollars to more counseling. You can begin to make major changes in your life *right now*—before you put this book down and turn out the light for the night—but you have to face facts first: **you have a problem with rage**. All the awful words, the screaming, the pushing and shoving, the broken relationships, the blaming, the guilt and shame, and the excuses—lots and lots of excuses—it all fits a pattern. Maybe you don't want to believe it is all about you, and maybe it isn't really *all* about you. But the part where *you* scream and curse and break things and hurt people you love, that part is *all about you*. And people who behave like this have a serious problem. Sometimes they are called "rageaholics" because they seem to be addicted to anger. No matter what they try to do about it, they always seem to come back around to another rage event.

Like most people with a rage problem, you have tried all sorts of things in an attempt to get your life back to normal. Unfortunately, none of them worked, at least not for very long. But what did you do? You kept doing them anyway, just louder, longer, harder and faster. More apologies, more make-up presents, even more counseling, more heart-to-heart talks, more excuses, more explanations, followed by more outbursts. You learned one thing: *the more you do what you always did, the more you will get what you always got!* Aren't you tired of getting what you always got? Then the first thing to do is *to stop doing what you have always done!* In other words, whatever it is you have tried to do just flat isn't working, so doesn't it just make sense to **stop doing it?!**

First Thing to Do If You Are Stuck In A Hole? Stop Digging!

Now, freeze right there. Before we take one step toward introducing you to the material in this workbook—powerful stuff that is going to give you the traction you need to change your life—stop right here and soak in this mind-boggling suggestion. Did it ever occur to you that, instead of rummaging through your childhood to find explanations for your anger, and instead of having deep discussions in the middle of the night with your wife trying to help her understand why you have a good reason to be angry (which, by the way, always leads to more fights), you could just *stop doing those things* that are causing everyone so much pain in the first place? Well, that is the premise on which this workbook is based.

Here's why. A long time ago, probably about the same time you were learning your ABCs, you were also learning the ABCs of anger—and for you that meant Anger, Blame, and Criticism. How or why you learned it isn't the point here, but the fact is you developed a relationship to anger that hurts you and the people around you. So, in this workbook you are going to learn a new set of ABCs—*Abstain, Believe and Communicate*. And it all begins with a commitment to immediately **stop** doing the things that look and sound and feel like anger. Too simplistic? Too mechanical? Too hard? Not really, especially once you consider what fuels anger in the first place.

Getting All Steamed Up

During the early years of the 20th Century, Dr. Walter Cannon first introduced the idea of the "fight or flight" response as a way of describing the body's physiological responses to stressful, threatening events. Since that time, numerous studies have documented the remarkable physical changes that go on under the surface while we are experiencing emotions such as fear or anger. During these times, your sympathetic nervous system starts arming your body for a possible physical attack. Your muscles get tense, your blood pressure and heart rate go through the roof, your digestive system shuts down, and the chemistry affecting the processes in your brain actually become altered. It is kind of like heating up steam in a boiler to produce a high-level burst of energy. This is all for the purpose of getting you ready to fight as hard as you can or run as fast as you can. These changes are very useful on the battlefield, or even on the football field, but they cause nothing but problems at home or on the job. So, the trick is to find a way to shut down the boiler that is producing all that steam and pressure.

People who have difficulty distinguishing between being attacked by a roaring mountain lion and discussing family finances with their wives eventually end up in some sort of therapy sessions. We have already alluded to the fact that most of the time the way anger is dealt with in counseling is not helpful. One standard approach is to do a lot of talk therapy or insight therapy, where you examine your childhood or other events in the hope of finding and addressing the wounds that caused you to become chronically angry in the first place. There are two problems with this approach. First of all, it can actually make you *angrier* as you finally face some very sad truths about your past. But the bigger problem is that this process can take a long time; months, maybe even years. In the meantime, your wife (and maybe even a judge) wants something done *now*. Your window of opportunity right now may be measured in a matter of days, or, at the most, weeks. You can waste a lot of time talking and yet not really do anything to alleviate the rage—shut down the boiler—that still comes out of nowhere without warning and overwhelms you. You need a solution *now*.

Another approach is the "Build-up/Blow-up Theory of Anger." Although a lot of models fit under this heading, the one thing they all have in common is encouraging angry people to "let it all out." The idea is that yelling, screaming, crying, hitting pillows and lots of other creative ways of "expressing" anger (in safe, controlled settings, of course) will help to diffuse the anger and get rid of it permanently. As it turns out, this idea rarely ever solves the problem, especially for men with genuine rage issues.

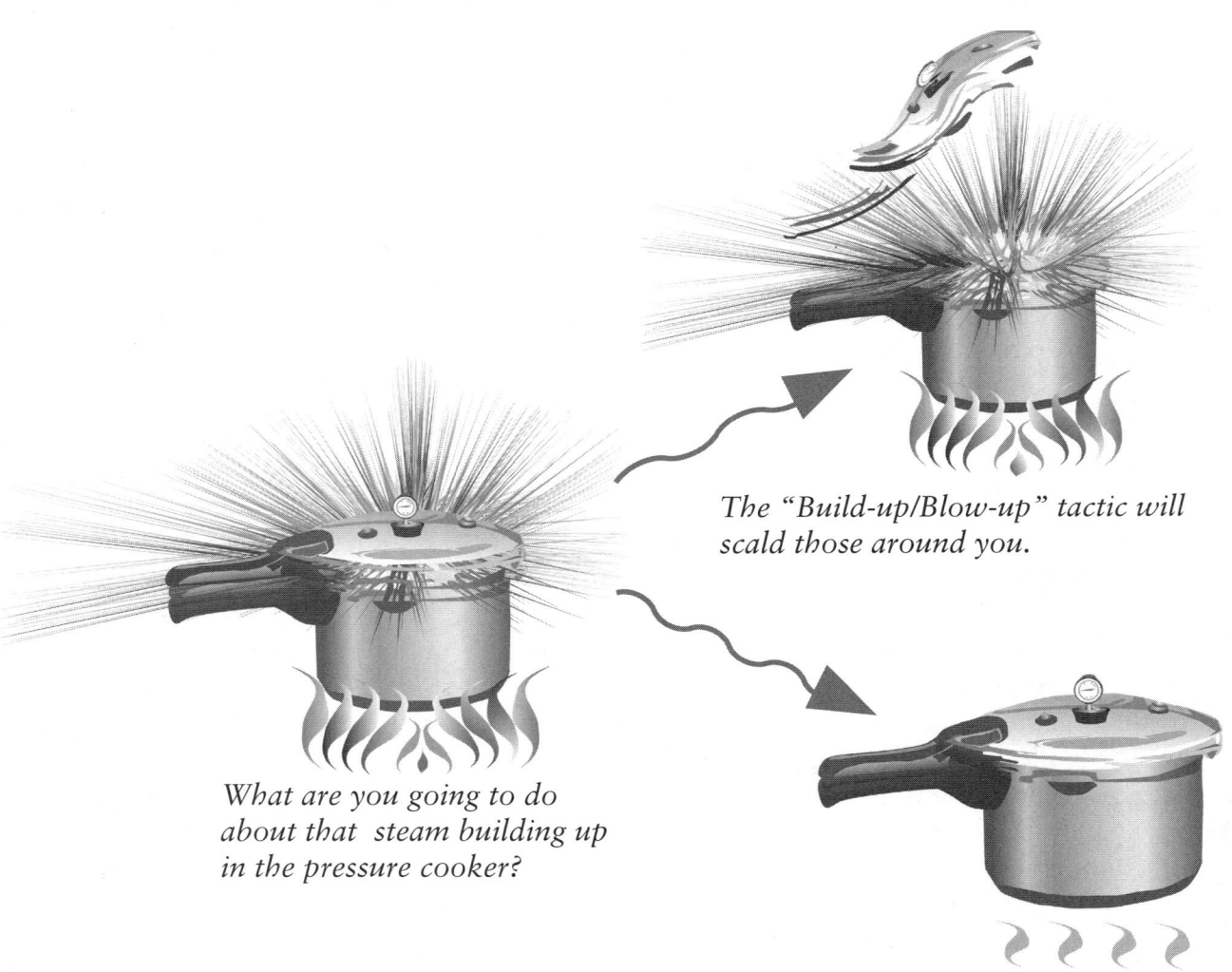

What are you going to do about that steam building up in the pressure cooker?

The "Build-up/Blow-up" tactic will scald those around you.

Try turning off the fire. No more steam, no more pressure.

Remember, we have an overheated boiler. Think of anger like the pressurized steam building up in a pressure cooker. The question is, how do we safely alleviate that pressure? Now, we *can* relieve the pressure by taking the lid off and letting all the steam come rushing out, but with what result? Anyone standing nearby is going to get scalded! But more than that, we haven't really solved the problem. The trouble isn't the lid on the top of the pan; it is the *fire* burning under the bottom of the pan! *Turn off the fire* and there is no more steam, no more pressure, no more danger.

That's why we are suggesting that the first thing you need to do is stop doing all those things you usually do when you are angry. You may not realize it yet, but all those things—the words, the tone of voice, the body language, the explanations and excuses, the arguing—are actually fueling the anger fire under your boiler. That fire keeps the steam building and the pressure rising. Your "fight or flight" system just keeps right on percolating. And the anger response just keeps growing. Do you want to get an immediate handle on your anger problems? Turn off the fire. Stop doing what you have always done.

Addicted to Rage

We are not suggesting that helping some people express their anger in safe, controlled ways is a bad idea; we are only saying that it doesn't help people with rage problems. Think of it like this: does it really make sense to take a keg of beer to an alcohol treatment center so that problem drinkers can "get it all out of their system?" In the same way that alcoholics are addicted to alcohol, "rageaholics" are *addicted to rage*. The more alcoholics drink, the more they want to keep drinking. Rage follows the same pattern: the more ragers rage, *the more they want to rage*. As anger builds in a rage addict, a combination of physiological processes and learned behaviors sets up a cascade effect that pushes him to harsher, more aggressive, even violent, expressions of anger. This is why the very first rule you need to learn, **right now**, is that when you are angry, **don't say anything!** When a rage addict starts talking about his anger, it only makes him angrier, like turning up the fire under the pressure cooker. *Shutting up* is like *shutting off* the flame under the pressure cooker. It can help to prevent a rage event by giving the body's physiological processes a chance to return to normal.

The Telltale Signs of Rageaholism

That's right—we are calling this relationship with rage an addiction! In order for a behavior to be classified as addictive, it has to follow a standard pattern: self-stimulation; compulsion, obsession; denial; withdrawal and craving syndrome; and unpredictable behavior. Drug use and alcoholism both fit this pattern, and in many cases, so does anger.

Self-Stimulation—Once a rageaholic starts to express anger, it triggers an ever-intensifying anger cascade.

Compulsion—Essentially, this is the inability to stop expressing anger once you start an episode. Rageaholics continue to rage compulsively in spite of the negative consequences that will inevitably follow. Whenever we can no longer control how much or when we rage, we have crossed the line into addiction.

Obsession—Anger addicts are very often preoccupied with resentment and fantasies about revenge. It often seems uncontrollable; thoughts of being wronged and "getting even" begin to overwhelm conscious thought, crowding out all other lines of thinking. Eventually, the focus of life becomes chronically *revenge oriented*. Anger is now driving the bus.

Denial—At this point, rageaholics are trapped in their addiction by a nifty bit of mental judo called denial. You might find yourself saying, "My problem isn't anger, my problem is *her*!" Instead of focusing on the terrible and destructive nature of your own actions, you shift focus to what the other person did. Jesus once said, "Take the log out of your own eye before trying to take the speck out of your neighbor's eye." But a rageaholic can't do that. He can't risk letting go of his anger.

Withdrawal and Craving—Anger addicts are so dependent on rage that they often experience symptoms of withdrawal as they go through their "detox" period. Ragers who abstain from expressions of anger for 90 days are usually then free of old anger patterns, but getting through that 90 days can be a challenge. During this detox phase, ragers report increased struggles with depression. And they also report indulging in something called "rescue fantasies." Simply put, they are hoping for an excuse to get really angry for a legitimate reason, like rescuing someone who is being threatened. Anything to get back that old exhilarating feeling.

Unpredictable Behavior—Just as an alcoholic can't predict what is going to happen when he takes a drink, a rageaholic can't ever predict when an expression of anger will rocket out of control. For an addict, there is really no such thing as an appropriate expression of anger because you can't really predict what will happen next.

You Talkin' To Me?

Let's be clear about one thing: this workbook is designed for that small percent of the population that has rage or violence problems. Not everyone needs this program, but if you are addicted to anger, nothing else is likely to help. You already know this to be true because you have tried everything you can think of and things just keep getting worse. If you are an anger addict, expressing anger will not do anything but cause more pain and get you deeper into the doghouse. So, the only question now is: are you an anger addict? Let's find out. Answer the following questions as "*true*" or "*false*." Be more honest and more courageous than you have ever been in your whole life. There is a lot riding on your ability to tell the truth right now. You aren't going to fool anybody but yourself.

ANGER SELF-ASSESSMENT TEST

T F 1. I've had trouble on the job because of my temper.
T F 2. People say that I fly off the handle easily.
T F 3. I don't always show my anger, but when I do, look out.
T F 4. I still get angry when I think of the bad things people did to me in the past.
T F 5. I hate lines, and I especially hate waiting in line.
T F 6. I often find myself engaged in heated arguments with the people who are close to me.
T F 7. At times, I've felt angry enough to kill.
T F 8. When someone says or does something that upsets me, I don't usually say anything at the time, but later I spend a lot of time thinking of cutting replies I could and should have made.
T F 9. I find it very hard to forgive someone who has done me wrong.
T F 10. I get angry with myself when I lose control of my emotions.
T F 11. I get aggravated when people don't behave the way they should.
T F 12. If I get really upset about something, I have a tendency to feel sick later (frequently experiencing weak spells, headaches, upset stomach or diarrhea).
T F 13. When things don't go my way, I "lose it."
T F 14. I am apt to take frustration so badly that I cannot put it out of my mind.
T F 15. I've been so angry at times I couldn't remember what I said or did.
T F 16. Sometimes I feel so hurt and alone that I've thought about killing myself.
T F 17. After arguing with someone, I despise myself.
T F 18. When riled, I often blurt out things I later regret saying.
T F 19. Some people are afraid of my bad temper.
T F 20. When I get angry, frustrated or hurt, I comfort myself by eating or using alcohol or other drugs.
T F 21. When someone hurts me, I want to get even.
T F 22. I've gotten so angry at times that I've become physically violent, hitting other people or breaking things.
T F 23. I sometimes lie awake at night thinking about the things that upset me during the day.
T F 24. People I've trusted have often let me down, leaving me feeling angry or betrayed.
T F 25. I'm an angry person. My temper has already caused lots of problems, and I need help changing it.

Reprinted with permission. © 2002 Newton Hightower, *Anger Busting 101*

Determining Your Score

Count the number of times you circled "T."

Write down that number.

My Self-Assessment Anger Score: _____   (Date: _____)

If you answered true to 10 or more of these questions, you have a problem with anger that needs to be addressed immediately. If you answered true to 5 questions, you are about average, but you could probably still benefit from some of the techniques discussed in this workbook. (If you want or need a more thorough and comprehensive assessment of your anger profile, you can get a psychologist to give you what is known as the STAXI-2 test. It is the most well-known and reliable instrument currently available for revealing details about your anger expression style.)

One Small Step for You, One Big Step for Your Future

So, the results have been tabulated. What will you do next? Maybe you still have doubts that you are really a rageaholic. But obviously there are important people in your life who think you need to do something, regardless of the label. Two things are certain: 1) If you don't do something now, things will not get better, and 2) this workbook will help you learn things that can help you to change right now. Why not commit to working through the steps in this book, and at least see where it might lead you?

One of the best ways to get started is to promise yourself and your spouse right now to stop doing those things that have put you in the doghouse. In the next section you will learn all about what this means, but right now you can take a step in the right direction by reading, signing and following the promises outlined below.

A Pledge to Change Starting Right Now

Beginning today, I promise myself and my spouse that I will:

❏ Stop trying to explain or make excuses for my angry outbursts

❏ Stop speaking when I am angry

❏ Not spend one second arguing with my wife

❏ Find truth in whatever she says to me

❏ Tell her she is right, with no "buts"

❏ Do the assignments in this workbook, and follow the instructions to the very last detail.

_____   _____
                Signature   Date

Witnessed by:

_____   _____
                Signature   Date

"HE'S A VERY ANGRY YOUNG MAN. I SHOULD KNOW.
I HAD TIGHT SHOES WHEN I WAS A KID."

PART I

A Recovery Plan for Angry Men

Bob continued to yell at other drivers long after he arrived home.

CHAPTER 1
Putting on the Brakes

Jerry and Carla, both 29 years old, have been married for five years, and it seems as though they have spent four of those years arguing. The arguments really started when they were dating; they usually got loud, but only once did it escalate to violence – Jerry shoved Carla into the side of the car after the argument that started over dinner at a restaurant got worse out in the parking lot. He apologized, she forgave him, and he proposed marriage the next week. For a while it looked as if everything would be smooth sailing. Of course, it wasn't. Everything about the wedding turned into an argument, the honeymoon was one big argument, and that pretty much set the tone for the marriage. Jerry would be fine until Carla said something or did something that set him off. He would rage, maybe break something, apologize, replace whatever he broke and promise to do better from then on. He seemed to be genuinely sorry, and he was really sweet after that, maybe for as long as a couple of weeks. But then something else would set him off. The more Carla tried to talk to him about it, the angrier and more out of control he seemed to get. Lately, there had been several incidents of shoving and slapping. Carla had done her share of yelling and shoving; she was getting pretty good at giving as good as she got. But she hated it; she hated being trapped in this kind of marriage, and there were plenty of days where she found herself hating Jerry. The trip to the therapist was her last hope. Something had to change soon. Thank goodness they didn't have any children yet.

The therapy session started out in typical fashion.

Therapist: *Okay, why doesn't somebody tell me why we are here.*

Carla:	I'll go first, I guess. After all, coming to see you is kind of my idea. We just seem to be fighting all the time. We will start having what I think is a normal conversation and then, I don't know, Jerry just kind of freaks. Pretty soon he is yelling and calling me names and …
Jerry:	(interrupting) Wait a minute! Why did you leave out the part where you start whining and complaining about practically everything under the sun? Don't try to make this all my fault!
Carla:	Honey, I know it is not all your fault, but you scare me when you start getting angry. Honestly, I don't know what's going on with you any more. Why can't you just back off and let us have a discussion like normal …
Jerry:	(Interrupting again – to therapist) See what I mean! She blames everything on me. (voice tense and rising) Listen, Carla, when are you going to learn to stop telling me how to run my life? I have had just about all of your BS I can stand! (to therapist) Can't you make her understand that she is driving me nuts? She never listens to me!
Therapist:	Okay, everybody settle down here. Take a deep breath and let's try to refocus. I think I have a pretty good picture of what has been going on. Jerry, when Carla called to set up this appointment she told me two things: she still loves you, and she is ready to leave you.
Jerry:	Yeah, I know she says that all the time. It's just one of her games.
Therapist:	Actually, Jerry, I get the definite impression that she is serious, and based on what I have seen so far, I can't say I blame her. I've been going over the anger questionnaire you filled out in the waiting room before you came in, and even without Carla's input here, it seems clear to me that you might be a nice guy at heart, but when you are angry you are probably not a nice guy at all. You may even be a dangerous guy at times. And it is about to cost you your marriage. So here is my question for you: Do you really want to save this marriage and help to make it better?
Jerry:	Hell! Of course I do. Why do you think I am paying you all this money to sit here and let you both insult me!
Therapist:	A simple yes or no would have been just fine. I'll take that as a yes. Now, I don't want to waste your time and I certainly don't want you wasting my time. If I could tell you something to do starting right now that would begin to break this cycle of fighting and blaming, and start you on the way to having a better marriage, would you be willing to give it a shot?
Jerry:	I don't know, I guess so. As long as it isn't something girly or ridiculously expensive.

Therapist: *No problem there, Jerry. It is very simple and it won't cost you a dime. What I want you to do, starting now, and continuing for the next 90 days, is to stop talking the minute you notice that you are angry about anything. Jerry, you can break the cycle of anger and fighting by just learning to* **shut up.**

Abstain From These Behaviors

As you can imagine, Jerry was skeptical at first, just as you may be right now. Most people take a little convincing and a lot of practice before they get the Big Picture behind this whole idea of abstaining from angry behaviors. To some guys, it seems like a cop-out, or a wimp-out. It might feel like you are giving people a free pass to walk all over you. But here's the deal: *anger addicts can't control their anger*. The only option you have is to *stop expressing it*. You must **slam on the brakes** now if there is to be any hope of saving your relationships and/or your job and beginning to build a more satisfying life for yourself. Eventually, you will have a chance to learn a different way to solve problems and resolve conflict. However, for now, it is better to "lose" an argument than to lose your family or your job, or both. So, let's look at the list of 16 separate things that a rageaholic must *stop doing* in order to turn out the fire under the anger pressure cooker.

1. STOP SPEAKING.

Silence is the all-time, fail-proof safest action to take when we feel rage well up inside of us. In the middle of a budding disagreement or a frustrating situation, you probably tell yourself things like, "I'm not going to just sit her and let her talk to me that way!" Instead, start telling yourself something like, "Don't go there, buddy. Just take a deep breath and keep driving." Even if your wife wants to draw you into a dialogue (that could lead to an argument), stay silent. If she asks if you are mad at her, respond as casually as possible, with something like, "Not in the least. I'm just happy to be alive and in love with you." Remind yourself that silence doesn't mean you have stopped listening. It means that you are in control of your anger.

2. STOP STAYING.

Again, this is very simple: when you feel the anger starting to build inside, leave the scene quickly and quietly. You should begin to monitor your anger signs to become aware of your internal anger states. Think of a scale of 0 – 10, with zero meaning no anger and ten equaling rage. Once you have reached five or higher, it is time to evacuate the area. If you get to eight, it may be too late. Learn to take "time-outs." Leave the scene and don't come back until you have calmed down, and make sure not to come back until your wife has calmed down, too.

3. STOP STARING.

Maybe the word we should use here is glaring, because that is really what we are talking about. Angry people are very good at striking out in anger simply by bearing down on others with the old "evil eye" in order to make it very clear that "I've got you in my sights." Don't stare when you are angry. Look at the floor, look at the ceiling, look anywhere, but don't stare at the other person. This can provoke a confrontation and it will only turn up the fire under your pressure cooker.

4. Stop interrupting.

Cutting off someone else in order to get your own point across or to defend yourself is another way to stoke that angry fire. Train yourself not to interrupt others. Also, if someone interrupts you, **you must allow it.** Instead of standing your ground, go back to rule one: Abstain from speaking. If you don't think you can do that, move on to rule two — leave.

If you are successful at implementing these first four new behaviors, people will notice the difference. You will be well on your way to controlling your anger addiction. These next steps will help you reinforce and maintain that progress.

5. Stop cursing.

This isn't a religious or a moral issue; it is a survival issue! Cursing has been consistently correlated with increased heart rate, blood pressure problems, and coronary disease in medical studies over the past 50 years. If you don't curse, you won't be firing up that pressure cooker. Abstaining from profanity will immediately reduce the amount of anger going on inside of you. Saying "Gee, whiz" definitely has a lower anger response than "&$*%%#*!" If you have been cursing for years just out of habit, this will take some practice, but it will also make an immediate and noticeable difference.

6. Stop name-calling.

There is really not very much difference between cursing and name-calling. They both are aggressive, insulting and, most of all, they both stoke that anger fire. So stop calling people names, and not just vile, crude names; stop using any term that is in any way derogatory or demeaning. Even terms like "stupid" and "crazy" are out. And don't try to excuse the use of such words by saying you were only teasing. People around you don't know when you are teasing and when you are making a dig at them. Name-calling is always destructive. Stop it.

7. Stop Threatening.

You know what this is referring to. Does "I'm warning you, Wanda, one of these days you are going to push me too far" sound familiar? Subtle or overt threats to leave or hurt are terrorizing to your partner. They also play right into the anger rush that makes you feel tough and in control. This can fire up the pressure cooker in a hurry. Don't risk it. Don't do it.

8. Stop pointing.

We usually point because we are trying to … well, make a point. But during an argument the point usually has something to do with threatening or intimidating someone. It can escalate an argument and elevate your anger level. Keep your hands in your pockets or your lap.

9. **STOP YELLING, RAISING YOUR VOICE, OR TALKING IN A MEAN TONE.**

Tone of voice is one of the quickest ways to communicate anger. The meaning to the other person is unmistakable. You may claim to be simply explaining yourself, or raising your voice just a little in order to get her attention. But it doesn't really matter, it is still threatening and intimidating. And it feeds your anger cycle. Start monitoring your tone and volume, using a scale of 0 – 10 (where zero equals silence). Anytime you get above three, it is time to turn it down. If you aren't sure how you are sounding, allow family or friends to point it out. And when they do, instead of protesting, excusing or explaining, just say, "Thanks for pointing that out." Then turn down the volume.

10. **STOP BEING SARCASTIC. STOP MOCKING.**

This is one of the classic elements of passive-aggressive anger, where you can get a dig in at someone and then claim to just be kidding, or trying to make a point or whatever. Just like name calling, it is disrespectful, hurtful and can cause real damage. And it derives from the same anger pressure cooker that has caused you so much trouble. Cut the sarcasm and cool the flame.

11. **STOP THROWING THINGS, SLAMMING DOORS, OR BANGING WALLS.**

Seems like this should be a no-brainer doesn't it? What could you do to jump start your anger cycle quicker than flexing those muscles and whacking something? Don't call it "letting off steam." Don't say it doesn't really hurt anyone. Don't slam. Don't bang. Don't throw. Just don't do it.

12. **STOP ALL NON-AFFECTIONATE TOUCHING.**

It is unacceptable to touch in anger, including any kind of aggressive touching like pushing or holding. It is also a bad idea. If the police are called and there are bruises evident from your attempt to "just hold her down until she calmed down," you could win a free trip downtown in a police car. Get a grip on your anger and quit grabbing other people. No touching when angry.

13. **STOP TELLING HERO STORIES.**

Do you realize that every time you tell someone about how you really chewed out somebody else or zinged someone good with a cutting remark, you are also reloading your anger reservoir? You may think of yourself as a hero, standing up for yourself against someone who was raining on your parade, but the truth is you are just an anger junkie looking for a quick fix. Stop the stories.

14. **STOP SIGHING, CLUCKING OR ROLLING YOUR EYES.**

This is more passive-aggressive anger behavior. Since it doesn't seem to be *overtly* destructive or mean-spirited, you think you can get away with it. But it is still a way to signal that you are tired of putting up with someone. It can fuel anger responses in yourself and your spouse. Let it go.

15. Stop criticizing and lecturing.

This can also be one of those expressions of passive-aggressive anger that allows you to get under someone else's skin without having to take responsibility for your actions. It is not your job to "help" your wife or your kids improve by pointing out all of their shortcomings. And it can lead to more arguments. And you know what that can lead to.

16. Stop speeding. Start "recovery driving."

Anger addicts are generally angry drivers. Impatient, aggressive, critical driving is no way to prepare yourself for a peaceful night at home. Your pressure cooker can be pretty well stoked by the time you hit the front door. Changing the way you drive can be the first step to changing your relationship to anger. Follow these rules for what is called "recovery driving."

1. Drive within 5 mph of the speed limit at all times.
2. If you drive more than 5 mph over the speed limit, then drive under the speed limit for the next 10 minutes.
3. No honking of the horn in anger.
4. Once the other driver sees you, stop honking.
5. Stop on yellow lights.
6. If someone wants to get in front of you, let him in and smile.
7. Avoid eye contact when another driver is angry at you.
8. Make no critical comments about anyone else's driving.
9. Abstain from cursing, banging the steering while, or shaking a fist while driving.

Making It Personal

Now that we have laid out the strategy for abstaining from angry behaviors, the next step is to figure out what role each of these behaviors might be playing in our lives on a regular base. We also want to determine how intensely these behaviors might be affecting us and those around us. Remember, we are looking for ways to cool the fire under that pressure. So let's start out with a picture of that pressure cooker.

Take a moment to study the picture of the pressure cooker below. If you are like most anger addicts, you already have a pretty good idea of the kinds of things that really tic you off: arguments over money with your wife, kids being rebellious, irritation with supervisor at work, disagreements with wife over relationship with her parent, etc. You know what is on your list. Now, on the blanks inside the diagram, list as many of these issues and events as you can possibly think of. If you use up the blanks, starting writing under, over or around the picture and out to the edges of the page.

Things that really make me angry:

Now, from your perspective, this is a list of the real problems. Have you ever said to yourself that if all these things would go away, your problems with anger would go away as well?

But not so fast. Do you suppose it might be possible that there are some men, maybe even some couples, who could discuss and work through problems like these without yelling, shoving, name-calling and the like? If that is true for some people, then doesn't it make sense that the things you put in the picture above might not really be telling the whole story? Is there something else that is really providing the heat for your pressure cooker?

Let's look at another picture of an empty pressure cooker. This time, fill in the empty blanks by listing any of the 16 "banned" behaviors that you can recall using during any of your anger events (even if it might have only been once, as far as you know). To help you, here is the list of banned behaviors again, slightly reworded:

- Speaking when angry
- Staying when angry
- Staring when angry
- Interrupting for any reason when angry
- Cursing any time, for any reason
- Name calling, any time for any reason
- Threatening
- Pointing
- Yelling, raising your voice, talking in a mean tone
- Mocking and/or being sarcastic
- Throwing things, slamming doors, banging walls
- Non-affectionate touching
- Telling "hero stories"
- Sighing, clucking or rolling eyes
- Criticizing and/or lecturing
- Speeding

Now using this list to fill in the blanks in the diagram below.

Behaviors I do when I am angry:

_____
_____
_____
_____
_____

After you have filled in the blanks to the best of your knowledge, ask your spouse or another close family member or friend to double check this list, just to make sure you didn't leave anything out. We are not questioning your honesty here, just your memory. Anger addicts very often simply don't recall what they do during an anger event, and they certainly can't see how it looks to the person on the other end. After your list has been verified and/or amended, it is time to take a long hard look at what has been going on.

Now, pause for a moment and look at each of these charts one more time. The first one lists items that you *think* have been causing your problems. The second diagram lists the set of behaviors that are *really doing the most damage* to you and those around you. As you begin to eliminate the items in the second list, the issues in the first list may very well become much more manageable.

The ABCs of Working in this Workbook

In keeping with the theme of ABC – getting down to the basic building blocks of your recovery – we have organized the exercises in this workbook into a simple three-step process that you will follow in each chapter – **Assess, Break through,** and **Chart progress.** In each step, you will work to customize the things you are learning, and design your own road to recovery. As we have already noted, there is a role in this process for your spouse or another close friend or family member to play. A word to the wise: try to get past the normal awkwardness of enlisting their help and just be glad they are willing to be available to you. This isn't about trying to embarrass you or punish you, this is about supporting you and helping you get to a better place in your life and your relationships. There are no winners and losers. If all work together, we will all be winners.

Assess Your Relationship to the 16 Banned Behaviors

Let's begin by reviewing one more time the list of the 16 behaviors to abstain from, except this time we are going to try to grade the frequency and the intensity of the way you express each of these behaviors when you are angry. Study the list below. Begin by putting a check mark in front of the box of each of the behaviors that you listed in your second pressure cooker diagram. Next, rate how frequently you engage in this behavior when you are angry by putting a circle around the letter that best describes your behavior pattern, with

> A = Always
> O = Often
> S = Sometimes
> R = Rarely

Finally, rate the intensity of the behavior. This has to do with the force or the effect of the behavior. Or put another way, it describes how the impact of this behavior causes the anger event to get worse or become more damaging. Circle the number that best applies, with

> 5 = Extremely destructive
> 4 = Very destructive
> 3 = Definitely a problem
> 2 = Mild problem
> 1 = Irritating

Banned Behavior Check List

Banned Behavior	Frequency	Intensity
❑ Speaking when angry	A O S R	5 4 3 2 1
❑ Staying when angry	A O S R	5 4 3 2 1
❑ Staring when angry	A O S R	5 4 3 2 1
❑ Interrupting for any reason when angry	A O S R	5 4 3 2 1
❑ Cursing any time, for any reason	A O S R	5 4 3 2 1
❑ Name calling, any time for any reason	A O S R	5 4 3 2 1
❑ Threatening	A O S R	5 4 3 2 1
❑ Pointing	A O S R	5 4 3 2 1
❑ Yelling, raising your voice, talking in a mean tone	A O S R	5 4 3 2 1
❑ Mocking and/or being sarcastic	A O S R	5 4 3 2 1
❑ Throwing things, slamming doors, banging walls	A O S R	5 4 3 2 1
❑ Non-affectionate touching	A O S R	5 4 3 2 1
❑ Telling "hero stories"	A O S R	5 4 3 2 1
❑ Sighing, clucking or rolling eyes	A O S R	5 4 3 2 1
❑ Criticizing and/or lecturing	A O S R	5 4 3 2 1
❑ Speeding	A O S R	5 4 3 2 1

Before we can accurately assess your score, allow your wife (or whoever is functioning as your sounding board in this recovery process) to also score your behavior using this exercise. Don't trust your memory or opinion if you really want an accurate picture of what has really been happening. A sheet for her is provided below:

Banned Behavior Check List — Partner's Perspective

Banned Behavior – Partner's Perspective	Frequency	Intensity
❑ Speaking when angry	A O S R	5 4 3 2 1
❑ Staying when angry	A O S R	5 4 3 2 1
❑ Staring when angry	A O S R	5 4 3 2 1
❑ Interrupting for any reason when angry	A O S R	5 4 3 2 1
❑ Cursing any time, for any reason	A O S R	5 4 3 2 1
❑ Name calling, any time for any reason	A O S R	5 4 3 2 1
❑ Threatening	A O S R	5 4 3 2 1
❑ Pointing	A O S R	5 4 3 2 1
❑ Yelling, raising your voice, talking in a mean tone	A O S R	5 4 3 2 1
❑ Mocking and/or being sarcastic	A O S R	5 4 3 2 1
❑ Throwing things, slamming doors, banging walls	A O S R	5 4 3 2 1

(Continued)
Banned Behavior – Partner's Perspective   Frequency   Intensity

- ☐ Non-affectionate touching   A O S R   5 4 3 2 1
- ☐ Telling "hero stories"   A O S R   5 4 3 2 1
- ☐ Sighing, clucking or rolling eyes   A O S R   5 4 3 2 1
- ☐ Criticizing and/or lecturing   A O S R   5 4 3 2 1
- ☐ Speeding   A O S R   5 4 3 2 1

Now, go line by line and compare your score with the way your partner scored you.

Note any areas where there is a significant variation in the score. For instance, it is probably okay if you gave yourself a 3 and she gave you a 4 on sarcastic remarks. But if she gave you a 5 and you gave yourself a 2, then there is a good chance that you have been minimizing or ignoring the seriousness of the problem. For the purpose of the rest of the exercises in this workbook, wherever there is a variation between the way you score yourself and the way your partner scores you – even a minor one – use your partner's score.

After reviewing the scores, go back and *underline the 5 behaviors* that you believe are causing the most damage or creating the biggest problems for you and those around you. Make the selection based on frequency and intensity, i.e., those that occur Always or Often, and which also have a rating of 4 or 5. Double-check this list with your partner. She may also want to include a behavior that has a lower intensity rating, but which happens so often that it creates a lot of problems. Or there may be a behavior that doesn't happen all the time, but the damage that occurs when it does happen is so great that it needs to be addressed in a special way. Again, if there is a difference of opinion, go with the five behaviors that she deems most urgent. List those behaviors below:

Top five behaviors to work on:

_____

_____

_____

_____

BREAK THROUGH *to safer, smarter behavior patterns*

Now that we are through the ASSESSMENT phase, the next step is to take the information we have collected and design a strategy to put the brakes on these behaviors for good. We'll BREAK THROUGH to safer, smarter behavior patterns. Please remember that abstaining from **all 16** of the behaviors in this chapter is critical if you are to break through your anger addiction. We are giving special attention at the moment to the five behaviors that seem to be doing the most damage, *but that doesn't mean it is okay to slack off on abstaining from the other 11*. As a matter of fact, a lot of men will actually need to go back and repeat the exercises we are about to study, using the next set of 5 behaviors ranked just below the top five in terms of causing problems. And, depending on just how out of control things have been, you might even need to repeat these exercises for all 16 behaviors.

Remember, the goal in this chapter is for you to learn how to quickly and effectively ABSTAIN from these 16 behaviors. *You have to stop feeding the fire under your pressure cooker.* Let's begin by returning to the scene of the crime, in a manner of speaking. We want to get a good picture of the components of your anger events and how they come together.

Start by briefly summarizing all of the rage events that you have had during the past 6 to 8 weeks. Describe when each one happened, where it happened, who was involved, what the conflict was about, and what happened. For instance:

EVENT ONE

When: *It happened last Thursday, around bedtime.*

Where: *At home, in the bedroom, at least, that is where it started.*

Who was involved: *Just Karen and me.*

What the conflict was about: *She wanted me to promise to pick up the kids from school the next day because she had to take her mother to an important doctor's appointment, and I was trying to tell her that I already had a full plate at work and couldn't get off.*

What happened: *She got really whiney and accused me of only caring about work and I told her that she had no idea what I went through at work and she started crying and tried to walk out on me and I tried to hold her and make her sit down and finish talking. She jerked away from me and I grabbed her and she yelled at me to get away from her and I yelled at her and probably called her some names. At any rate I ended up screaming at her to just shut up and get over it or I was going to shut her up.*

Got the idea now?

So take as long as necessary to accurately and honestly fill in the worksheets below. We have provided space for five events. If you need more space, use extra sheets of paper. If you can't think of five events from the past six or eight weeks, please consult with your spouse before stopping at less than five.

Event One

When: _____

Where: _____

Who was involved: _____
_____

What the conflict was about: _____
_____

What happened: _____
_____
_____
_____
_____
_____

Event Two

When: _____

Where: _____

Who was involved: _____
_____

What the conflict was about: _____
_____

What happened: _____
_____
_____
_____
_____
_____

Event Three

When: _____

Where: _____

Who was involved: _____

_____

What the conflict was about: _____

_____

What happened: _____

_____

_____

_____

_____

Event Four

When: _____

Where: _____

Who was involved: _____

_____

What the conflict was about: _____

_____

What happened: _____

_____

_____

_____

_____

EVENT FIVE

When: _____

Where: _____

Who was involved: _____
_____

What the conflict was about: _____
_____

What happened: _____
_____
_____
_____
_____
_____

Now, we are going back to study each of these events one more time. This time, like a detective, we are looking for clues about your behavior. The first thing we want to identify is when in the course of each of these events you first noticed that you were starting to get angry. Were you already feeling tense about something before the encounter began? Did things start out calm and reasonably cordial until something was said or done that stirred feelings of anger, defensiveness, or frustration in you? To the best of your ability, think back through each of these events and try to pinpoint when you first felt the fire start sizzling under your pressure cooker.

EVENT ONE

I first noticed I was getting angry around the time that _____
_____
_____

EVENT TWO

I first noticed I was getting angry around the time that _____

_____

_____

EVENT THREE

I first noticed I was getting angry around the time that _____

_____

_____

_____

EVENT FOUR

I first noticed I was getting angry around the time that _____

_____

_____

EVENT FIVE

I first noticed I was getting angry around the time that _____

_____

_____

(If you had more than five anger events over the past 6-8 weeks, record your answers on a separate sheet of paper.)

The next step is very important. It would be very valuable to have some idea of what was playing on the channel inside your head while this conflict was building. We will call this your *internal monologue*, and it boils down to this simple question: What thoughts and reactions were you hearing on the inside while the anger scenario was developing on the outside? Learning to pay attention to this monologue and noticing where it is likely to lead you is a very important tool in your fight against anger addiction.

Let's go back to our earlier example on page 45. During the argument between Karen and her husband, what do you suppose might have been playing in his head? We can provide a pretty good guess. It probably sounded something like this:

Internal monologue for Karen's husband: *Why is she bringing this up now? I am really tired, I have to be at work at 7 am, and I don't even want to think about it! ... Now she is complaining and criticizing me, accusing me of not caring about the kids or her. She really has no clue about how much I sacrifice for this family ... Oh, God, now she is crying. She is going to wake up the kids and it is going to be my fault again ... Maybe if I can just get her to calm down ... I can't believe we are going through this again. I have to make her STOP!*

Now, review your five events and, to the best of your ability, record your internal monologue. (Remember, if you have more than five events, use a separate sheet of paper for the extra ones.)

EVENT ONE

Internal monologue: _____

_____

_____

_____

_____

_____

_____

_____

EVENT TWO

Internal monologue: _____

_____

_____

_____

_____

_____

_____

_____

EVENT THREE

Internal monologue: _____

_____

_____

_____

_____

_____

_____

EVENT FOUR

Internal monologue: _____

_____

_____

_____

_____

_____

_____

EVENT FIVE

Internal monologue: _____

_____

_____

_____

_____

_____

_____

The next step is to identify how many of the 16 banned behaviors you exhibited during each of these events. Review each again, and then list any occurrence of these behaviors in the blanks below. If you still aren't clear on what each of these behaviors is, refer to the list that starts back on pages 35-38. Be sure and let your spouse double check your list for accuracy.

To illustrate, let's refer again to our example of the argument between Karen and her husband (p. 45). The behaviors obviously evident in this event are:

Banned Behaviors by Karen's husband: *Kept talking, kept staying, name-calling, non-affectionate touching, screaming, threatening*

Now, record your answers below:

EVENT ONE

Banned Behaviors: _____ _____

_____ _____

_____ _____

_____ _____

_____ _____

EVENT TWO

Banned Behaviors: _____ _____

_____ _____

_____ _____

_____ _____

EVENT THREE

Banned Behaviors: _____   _____

_____   _____

_____   _____

_____   _____

_____   _____

EVENT FOUR

Banned Behaviors: _____   _____

_____   _____

_____   _____

_____   _____

_____   _____

EVENT FIVE

Banned Behaviors: _____   _____

_____   _____

_____   _____

_____   _____

_____   _____

_____   _____

(If you recorded more than five events during the past 6-8 weeks, list the behaviors from the remaining events on a separate sheet of paper.)

If you have made it this far, you are definitely working hard to make important changes in your life. And make no mistake about it, this is **hard** work! But hang in there; you are about to turn a very important corner here.

Writing a New Script

The next step is a little trickier. Now that we have identified areas where these banned events have been occurring, we need to go back and review these events one more time. What we are looking for now is *alternative ways to deal with the situation.*

By this we mean, something to do instead of staying in the argument or even staying in the room; something to do instead of screaming or name-calling; something to do that might have turned off the fire before things got out of hand.

For instance, let's go back to the example we started with on page 45. In this example, Karen's husband exhibited at least seven banned behaviors. He kept talking, he kept staying, and he used name-calling, non-affectionate touching, screaming, and threatening. In addition, his internal monologue was full of resentment. Instead of trying to understand Karen's need, instead of paying attention to the rising pressure in his anger pressure cooker, he was psyching himself up for a major blow-up with a lot of self-serving, self-pitying, self-righteous garbage.

What do you suppose might have happened to Karen's husband if he had stood up to *himself* (instead of Karen) and written a different monologue? What if he had told himself things like:

I know she isn't bringing this up because she plans to intentionally screw up my day tomorrow. Her mom is really sick and I know she needs help.

I could at least talk to Mark in the morning and see if he would cover for me for an hour. I can just go back and work an hour late.

What if, instead of just saying *"No! My plate is too full already,"* he had said, *"I'm not sure, honey. I will have to check with Mark in the morning and see if he can cover for me."*

What if, when she started to cry, he had said, *"Honey, I'm sorry for snapping at you. I really love you and I am just as concerned for your mom as you are. I can't make any promises yet, but I will do my best to work something out."*

And most important of all, when he first began to realize that his anger was starting to build, what if he had told himself, *"Be careful here, you are starting to get really touchy. You better quit talking about this right now and take a time out. Tell Karen you need to get a glass of milk and sit down and think for a minute, and leave the room, now.*

Now we want to rewrite the scripts on the five recent anger events that we have been studying. You have a pretty good idea of what happened, what your internal monologues were like, and the list of banned behaviors that occurred during the event. Your job at this point is to design a different strategy that you could have employed to replace the things that you actually did. You will completely rewrite your response. Begin by replacing your internal monologue with thoughts and instructions that would have helped you avoid an escalating anger event. Finish the exercise by making a list of safe behaviors that you could have used instead of the banned ones.

Remember, before you can safely and reasonably stand up *for* yourself, *you have to learn to stand up to yourself.* Start planning ways to take control of your anger, beginning right here and now!

Event One

Instead of thinking and saying the things I did, I could have told myself _____
_____
_____
_____

I could have said _____
_____
_____
_____

Now replace each of the banned behaviors you used with an action or a choice that would have helped to turn down the fire under your pressure cooker.

Instead of _____

I could have _____

Instead of _____

I could have _____

Instead of _____

I could have _____

Instead of _____

I could have _____

Instead of _____

I could have _____

EVENT TWO

Instead of thinking and saying the things I did, I could have told myself _____
_____
_____
_____

I could have said _____
_____
_____
_____

Now replace each of the banned behaviors you used with an action or a choice that would have helped to turn down the fire under your pressure cooker.

Instead of _____

I could have _____

Instead of _____

I could have _____

Instead of _____

I could have _____

Instead of _____

I could have _____

Instead of _____

I could have _____

Event Three

Instead of thinking and saying the things I did, I could have told myself _____
_____
_____
_____

I could have said _____
_____
_____
_____

Now replace each of the banned behaviors you used with an action or a choice that would have helped to turn down the fire under your pressure cooker.

Instead of _____

I could have _____

Instead of _____

I could have _____

Instead of _____

I could have _____

Instead of _____

I could have _____

Instead of _____

I could have _____

Event Four

Instead of thinking and saying the things I did, I could have told myself _____

_____

_____

_____

I could have said _____

_____

_____

_____

Now replace each of the banned behaviors you used with an action or a choice that would have helped to turn down the fire under your pressure cooker.

Instead of _____

I could have _____

Instead of _____

I could have _____

Instead of _____

I could have _____

Instead of _____

I could have _____

Instead of _____

I could have _____

EVENT FIVE

Instead of thinking and saying the things I did, I could have told myself _____

_____

_____

_____

I could have said _____

_____

_____

_____

Now replace each of the banned behaviors you used with an action or a choice that would have helped to turn down the fire under your pressure cooker.

Instead of _____

I could have _____

Instead of _____

I could have _____

Instead of _____

I could have _____

Instead of _____

I could have _____

Instead of _____

I could have _____

Failing to Plan is Planning to Fail

You will begin by visualizing and writing out three imaginary — but very possible — scenarios that contain high risk factors for developing into anger events. By now, you are probably highly aware of the issues, the people, and the situations that are usually involved in your rage outbursts. You should be pretty clear about the 16 behaviors to abstain from, and what to think and what to do instead. Your assignment is to describe a situation that you could find yourself in at any time, including time, place, people, and the basic source of the potential conflict. But instead of writing out what you have always done and said in previous situations, this time write down what you intend to do differently. Be sure to refer back to any of the previous worksheets that you have done to give yourself the pointers you need to make your new plan.

SCENARIO ONE

Time: _____

Place: _____

People involved: _____

Reason for conflict: _____

_____

_____

_____

Instead of doing what I have always done, this time I will:

Make myself aware of: _____

_____

_____

_____

I will tell myself: _____

_____

_____

_____

I will abstain from these behaviors: _____

_____

_____

I will choose to say the following safe things: _____

_____

_____

_____

I will make the following safe choices or take the following safe actions: _____

_____

_____

_____

Scenario Two

Time: _____

Place: _____

People involved: _____

Reason for conflict: _____

Chapter 1 • Putting on the Brakes

_____

_____

_____

Instead of doing what I have always done, this time I will:

Make myself aware of: _____

_____

_____

_____

I will tell myself: _____

_____

_____

_____

I will abstain from these behaviors: _____

_____

_____

I will choose to say the following safe things: _____

_____

_____

_____

I will make the following safe choices or take the following safe actions: _____

_____

_____

_____

_____

SCENARIO THREE

Time: _____

Place: _____

People involved: _____

Reason for conflict: _____

_____

_____

_____

Instead of doing what I have always done, this time I will:

Make myself aware of: _____

_____

_____

_____

I will tell myself: _____

_____

_____

_____

I will abstain from these behaviors: _____

_____

_____

I will choose to say the following safe things: _____

_____

_____

_____

_____

I will make the following safe choices or take the following safe actions: _____

_____

_____

_____

Plan Your Work and Work Your Plan

Congratulations! You now have something you can use to finally put out the fire under your anger. Now it is a matter of using it, before you lose it again. You may be familiar with the old business management adage, "plan your work and then work your plan." Your job for the next 90 days is to work the plan that you have built for yourself here. You have learned a lot of useful insights, tools, and skills that can definitely help you break through your addiction to anger. Now it is time to put them into practice in the real world.

CHARTING Your Progress

Old habits die hard. Old fears and old patterns don't melt away over night. And anytime we have to learn a new skill, we can expect to climb a steep learning curve before we are comfortable using it. The new things that you are learning may feel very strange to you right now. Even at this moment you may still be thinking that this can't possibly work. This whole process might seem to you to be about the same as jumping out of an airplane without a parachute – just a very bad, very risky idea. We are totally sympathetic to how you feel. We have been in the same place and had those same sick, plummeting feelings. A lot of guys have been right where you are, thinking the exact same things, but they have found the courage to take a leap of faith anyway. Some guys just had no choice; some guys were simply tired of getting what they always got; and a few guys were genuinely excited about finding a new way to live their lives. No matter how you are feeling, you can still take a leap of faith, too.

To help you monitor your progress over the next 90 days, we have provided a set of charts you can use to note the situations you face and how you handled them. It is not reasonable to expect that you will be able to instantly change every aspect of your anger patterns. But it is absolutely right to expect that it won't take much practice for you to begin to recognize that on the occasions when you are successful at following your plan, you will get a different, and better result.

Using the Progress Chart

This is very simple and straight-forward. The purpose is to simply document every time you slip back into one of the banned behaviors, record what happened, and assign a consequence for violating the guidelines you have established for your recovery. There are two lines for each day on the chart, in case there might be more than one incident to document on any particular day. Hopefully, those days will grow fewer and fewer as the weeks pass.

For each day on the chart, write "no" if there was no violation that day. If there was any kind of anger event at all, write "yes" and move to the next blank. Under "persons affected" list the name or names of those who were exposed to your anger. In the next blank write a very brief summary of what happened, i.e., "argued about kids after supper," "blew up at customer at work," etc. The next space is for you to record the number of each of the banned behaviors you used. Refer to the beginning of this chapter for the number that corresponds to each behavior. In the last blank, designate whatever consequence you have been assigned to compensate for your inappropriate behavior. You will learn more about consequences in Chapter 3. For now, all you need to know is that your wife or accountability partner will be responsible for suggesting the consequences. On any day that you both agree that there were no violations, you are also entitled to some sort of reward. Don't make it a big deal (unless it comes at the end of a week with no violations of any sort).

Using the Recap Sheet

You can use this tool to help you sort out what happened and why, following any time when you failed to stick to your recovery plan. There is a place to record what thoughts were going through your head, and a place for you to list the things you want to try to tell yourself next time. There is also a place for you to write down each of the behaviors you failed to abstain from, and a place to list the actions and choices you will try to follow next time. Finally, there is a space for you to summarize anything that you may have learned from this event that can help you to handle the next one better.

Don't worry about failing. Instead, focus on this definition of success: A man is a success who falls down six times but gets up seven times. It all comes down to this: If you don't quit, you can't lose.

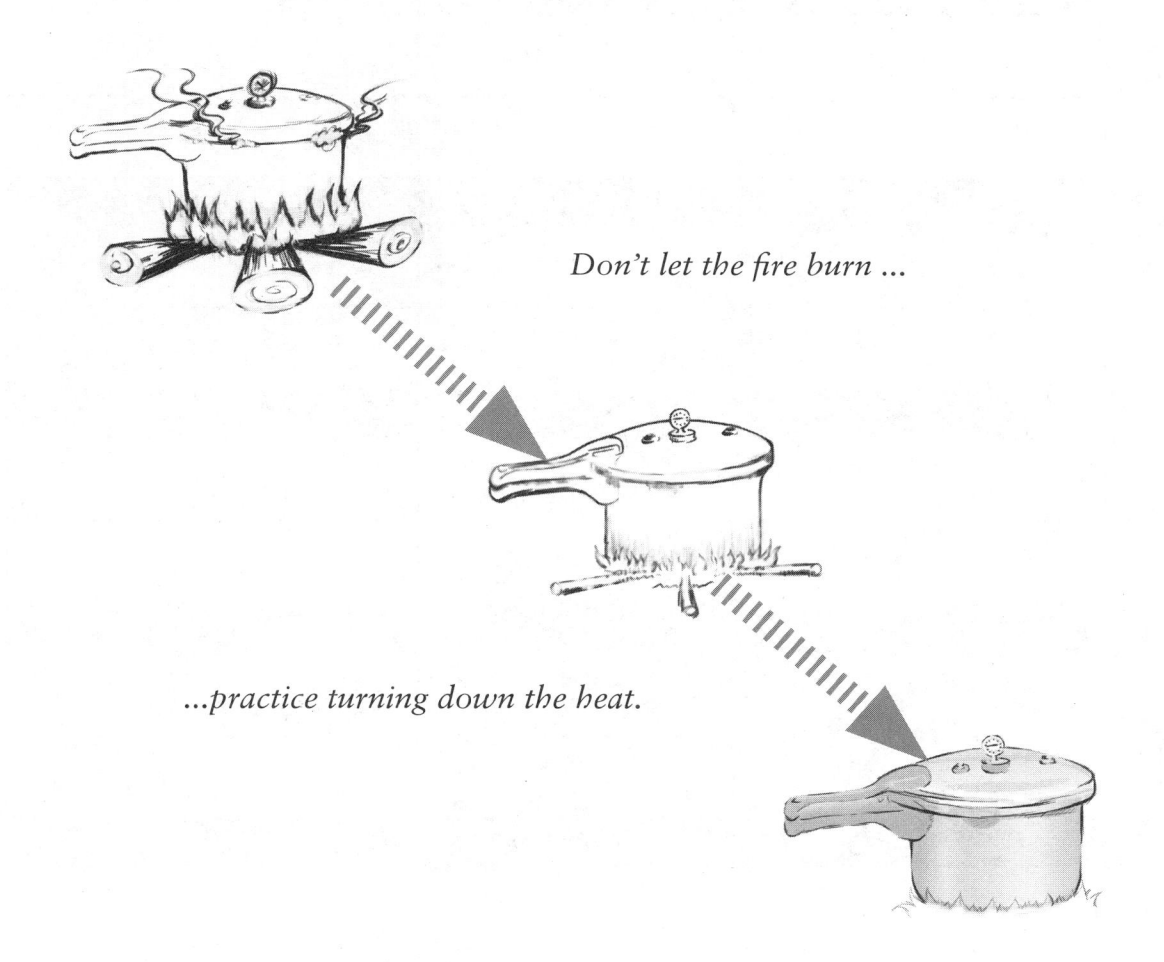

Don't let the fire burn ...

...practice turning down the heat.

Anger Busting Progress Chart

Week# _____
Date from _____ to _____

	☐ Y/N	☐ Persons Affected	☐ Summary of Event	☐ BB#	☐ Consequences/Rewards
SUNDAY					
Event 1					
Event 2					
MONDAY					
Event 1					
Event 2					
TUESDAY					
Event 1					
Event 2					
WEDNESDAY					
Event 1					
Event 2					
THURSDAY					
Event 1					
Event 2					
FRIDAY					
Event 1					
Event 2					
SATURDAY					
Event 1					
Event 2					

☐-*(Y/N) Was there a behavior violatioin? Yes/ No*   ☐-*(Persons Affected) Who was affected by the violation?*
☐-*(Event Summary) Briefly summarize the event*   ☐-*(BB#) From the list on pgs 35-38, write the # of the banned behavior*   ☐-*(Consequence/ Reward) Briefly note the consequences (positive or negative) from the event*

Anger Busting Recap Sheet

Select an event from the previous page (any of the events will do). Use the following fill-in-the blank questions to guide you in reviewing that event in a bit more detail.

Date of the Event: _____

During this event I was letting the following thoughts control me: _____
_____
_____
_____

What I could have told myself that would have been more helpful: _____
_____
_____
_____

Inappropriate Actions I failed to abstain from: _____
_____
_____

Better choices I will make the next time I am in this situation: _____
_____
_____
_____

What I need to learn from this event is: _____
_____
_____
_____
_____

"Take two, twice a day to help control rage. By the way, I put them in a child-proof bottle and overcharged you."

CHAPTER 2
A Check-Up from the Neck Up

Kelsey, 37, and Michael, 39, had been having one of those marathon, non-stop arguments for days — the kind where even when you are not talking you are still fighting. Of course, this situation wasn't unique to their 12-year marriage. It was pretty much standard practice for them to get into a conflict over something, which would lead to Michael screaming, name-calling and slamming things, followed by periods of silence that could last for days. Most recently, the issue seemed to be money (no surprise there) and how much time Michael was spending on work. Kelsey's hours had been cut back at the store, and they had really counted on that income to help cover the new mortgage payment. They had refinanced the house to pay off credit cards and pay for Shelly's braces, and now their backs were against the wall ... again! So Michael was scrambling to pick up all the overtime he could, plus repairing and upgrading computers for friends on the side. He wasn't home much, and when he was, he was either busy or tired. And when Michael was busy or tired, he had a very short fuse.

About three days ago, Kelsey had mentioned to him, very cautiously, that she and the kids (Shelly, 11, and Patrick, 9) were really missing him and hoping that they could spend time together doing something fun as a family on the weekend. Michael responded with a list of jobs that he absolutely had to finish before Monday and dismissed any week-

end activities as completely out of the question. When Kelsey began to plead with him to clear just a few hours, that little straw broke the camel's back. Michael ripped into her for over 10 minutes about all that he was doing to keep this family financially solvent, reminding her that this was her own stupid fault for having such a stupid job at such a stupid store and wasn't there anyone around here that appreciated hard work anymore? After unleashing his very loud, very harsh broadside, he stormed out of the house, slamming the door behind him. Retreating to his workshop, he stayed there, working of course, for the rest of the night.

And so for the past three days it was like living in Antarctica. Kelsey and Michael spoke to each other in three-word sentences and the kids walked on eggshells when their dad was in the room, which wasn't that often. The pain and sadness in Kelsey's face said all that needed to be said, anyway. Michael's face looked like it had been carved out of Mt. Rushmore. Finally, on the third day, today, Michael came home with a kind of different look in his eyes; a little bit scared, a little bit sheepish, and maybe just a little bit apologetic. He took her into their bedroom, where they both sat down on the edge of the bed. With speech that was halting and quiet, he began this conversation:

Michael: Honey, I have been doing some thinking today and ... well ... (his voice trailed off for a second).

Kelsey: About what?

Michael: Uh, I just wanted you to know that I think you were probably right the other day, about me working too much and all. And ... well, ... I was wrong to act the way I did. I'm still not sure how much time I can clear out on Saturday, but I am going try to find a way to free up at least half of the day. Go ahead and plan whatever you think would be fun. I really do want to be with you and the kids.

Kelsey: (after a long, astonished pause) Michael, I don't know what to say; well, besides thank-you and that sounds wonderful. I just have one question ... what made you change your mind.

Michael: (taking a long, deep breath) Well, you are probably going to think this is pretty weird. You know that really churchy guy I work with named Bill? Nice guy, but I always thought he came on a little too strong about God and all. Anyhow, he could see I was really bummed out when I got to work the other day, and when he asked me what was wrong I was just mad enough to tell him. You know what he said? He said, "Mike, the quickest way to end a tug of war is to let go of your end of the rope." Isn't that strange? He also asked me to at least be open to the idea that God might help me if I would just ask. Well, I couldn't get that thought out of my mind. So, this morning, on the way to work, I told God I was willing to let go of my end of the rope, if he would just help me figure out what to do next. And here I am, letting go. You were right. I was wrong. I don't know exactly what to do now.

Kelsey: I do.

And she leaned over and gave him a huge, iceberg-melting kiss.

BELIEVE IN THESE PRINCIPLES FOR PEACE, HAPPINESS, AND PERMANENT CHANGE

Okay, we can't promise you that if you learn how to do all of the things we talk about in this workbook you will start getting lots of unsolicited, passionate kisses. But then again, your chances should certainly improve. The point is, men who rage end up wrecking their relationships, and when there is less destruction going on, there is more room for a lot of very nice things to happen. If you have made it this far, we are willing to bet that you are already finding that out for yourself.

But just because you have made it this far doesn't mean that you have reached the finish line. Now, before you start telling yourself things like, *"I have stopped raging. Isn't that good enough?"* try to understand this one thing: when you drain the old oil out of the crankcase, the job is only half done. Your car will run much better if you go ahead and put in oil that is new and fresh and clean. So, you have learned to stop raging. Congratulations. It is hard work and you deserve a lot of credit for hanging in there. And for some of you out there, that may really be all you need to do. But, if you want to be even more certain that you will not relapse into your old behaviors, and if you want to really boost your chances at a deeper and longer-lasting level of happiness in your life, then you are ready to take the next step.

There is an old saying in the addiction recovery movement that reminds us one major key to lasting recover is to *"get a check-up from the neck up."* In other words, most of our problems aren't caused by what is going on around us, they are caused by what is happening inside — inside our heads. The Book of Proverbs says it like this: *As a man thinks in his heart, so he is* (Proverbs 23:7 NASB). This is just a way of saying that what we believe in our minds tends to influence what we think and feel and choose. What we BELIEVE determines what we DO. Dr. Robert McGee, in his book *The Search For Significance*, says this another way. It isn't situations that cause our emotions; *it is what we believe about a situation that causes our emotions.* And it isn't any big secret that what activates our emotions usually controls our actions.

In chapter one we worked on ABSTAINING, which can produce some important changes from the *outside in*. But if you want to work on maintaining what you have gained, it is time to start working on what you BELIEVE and how you think. This will produce lasting changes from the *inside out*.

Getting Into the Spirit of Things

Most men, especially rage addicts, believe very strongly that they must be rough and tough and ***in control*** of every situation. Rage is one way to control situations by intimidating and controlling people around you. But now that you are beginning to control your angry outbursts, the next step in your growth will be to learn to *replace your belief in the* *need to control* with some beliefs that are more healthy and more helpful. This starts by believing in something that is bigger than you.

Yeah, we know. Most of you are uncomfortable talking about religion. Many times, religion refers to people using the idea of God and religious rules to control other people. People think of religion as a system that can be manipulated and used to manipulate. We're definitely **not** interested in another control system here. What we are talking about is *Spirituality*. You might say that spirituality is simply the idea of being open to the possibility of God touching your life. You don't need a system or a set of rules and doctrines for this; you only need to let go of your end of the rope and say, "Okay, I am open to the possibility of God touching my life." From that point on, just let things unfold naturally, and follow where it leads.

The purpose of this chapter then is to present to you a set of 20 spiritual values that are common to most of the world's spiritual belief systems. We strongly urge you to find ways to substitute these simple, universal truths for the old, control-driven values that have fueled your anger in the past.

1. PRACTICE SELF-RESTRAINT – DON'T ALWAYS EXPRESS YOURSELF.

You are already getting familiar with this idea because you have learned to abstain from the 16 destructive behaviors we discussed in Chapter One. But did you know that neurologists have discovered that changing behavior actually changes the way we think? Researchers using MRI technology can document changes in the electrochemical pathways in our brains when we work on changing an old behavior pattern. Self-restraint then actually teaches you to think in ways that are different, and better.

2. PRACTICE KINDNESS – NOT REVENGE.

For anger addicts, this will often involve acting and speaking in ways that are not exactly in line with our feelings. Sometimes other people get in our way or frustrate us with their needs and problems. At times like this, instead of just blurting out our angry thoughts and feelings, we will have to choose to talk and act in ways that are gentle, careful and respectful, even though what we really want to do is erupt and tell then exactly how we feel. The Bible talks about "speaking the truth in love" (Ephesians 4:15). It is important to be honest, but if you can't express your honesty with love and kindness, it is better to keep quiet for now.

3. PRACTICE BEING GRACIOUS – NOT CRITICAL.

How many people around you — spouse, children, friends, coworkers — have actually changed for the better because of your attempts to "help" them through constant critical remarks? Fear and negativity are terrible motivators. People may make some changes in order to appease you, but there is also a good chance that they will end up resenting you. They could even start digging an anger hole of their own. Occasionally it might be important to correct someone who is confused about something important, but not nearly as often as you think. Most of the time, what people need is encouragement, comfort and love. Do yourself and your loved ones a favor: resign from the job of pointing out what is wrong with them — especially your wife. Use the space below to write a resignation letter to God stating that you will no longer use criticism to "improve" the people around you.

Dear God:

_____

_____

_____

_____

_____

_____

_____   _____

Signed   Date

4. PRACTICE SELF-EXAMINATION – NOT BLAME.

What is the first thing you usually do when someone challenges you, criticizes you or puts you at risk of feeling like a failure? It is quite natural to feel defensive and to start a counter-offensive, maybe by pointing out where they are wrong, or where they have failed in the past. This is a sure fire way to get into an argument and, for anger addicts, that is a recipe for a rage disaster. Don't defend and don't explain. Instead, use these three magic words to defuse anger and build bridges:

"YOU ARE RIGHT."

You may not even be certain the other person is right, especially if it is your wife, but tell her she is right anyway. Then concentrate on finding the area where she is right — even if it is only a small percent — and work on improving that area instead of blaming someone else.

5. PRACTICE EMPATHY – NOT SELFISHNESS.

Whether we want to admit it or not, anger is usually rooted in selfishness. When we don't get our way, or when we feel attacked or accused, we get angry. Focusing on **"me"** and **"my feelings"** instead of being aware of the needs and feelings of our spouse, is caused by selfishness. It's a sure breeding ground for anger. During a delicate discussion, instead of trying to think of what you want to say next to stay on top, try listening — really **listening**— to what she is saying to you. Listen in order to understand her needs and feelings. Try saying something like this:

"What I hear you saying is … (and then try to repeat back her concern as close to word-for-word as you possibly can). Is that right?" Then **stop talking** and wait in silence for her reply.

6. PRACTICE SURRENDERING – NOT DOMINATING.

Every one of the world's major spiritual traditions has some version of the Golden Rule; you know – *treat others the way you would like to be treated*. Satisfaction and happiness rarely come from browbeating people into letting you have your way. Just like Michael learned in our opening story, very often the quickest way to peace and progress in relationships is to let go of your end of the rope. And trust God for the next step.

7. PRACTICE SERVICE TO OTHERS – NOT SELF-INTEREST.

This is another aspect of the Golden Rule. Thinking only in terms of power and profit and winning can become a very poisonous existence. In Israel there are two very large lakes, connected by the Jordan River. To the north, the Sea of Galilee is full of life, nurturing a thriving fishing industry and watering farms in every direction. The water from the Sea of Galilee flows out into the Jordan and continues on southward, finally emptying into what is known as the Dead Sea. This is the lowest piece of real estate on earth; so water flows in but it doesn't' flow out. The water slowly evaporates, leaving the Dead Sea full of salts and metals. Nothing lives in the Dead Sea and nothing lives around it. That is why they call it the Dead Sea. The Sea of Galilee is alive because it gives freely to everything and everyone all the time. At the other end, the Dead Sea is simply a victim of its own selfishness. It keeps everything, wins every hand, and just stays dead. Find a way to give back to others, to your family and your community. It sure beats the alternative.

8. PRACTICE DISCIPLINING YOURSELF – NOT "I HAVE TO HAVE MY WAY."

"The line dividing good and evil cuts through the heart of every human being. And who is willing to destroy a piece of his own heart?" – Alexander Solzhenitsyn

Alan Clements, in his book, *Instinct for Freedom*, chronicles his years as a Buddhist monk in Burma. One of the first things his teachers imparted to him was the distinction between four types of people in the world: Those who succumb to the forces of darkness, inside and out. Those who run from the dark forces. Still others who speak of confronting them. And those who engage these forces in battle — at all costs — even till death if need be.

As you have already learned if you have made it this far, the biggest and hardest battle is the one we must fight with ourselves. Remember, if you don't quit, you can't lose.

9. PRACTICE BEING PATIENT – NOT IMPULSIVE.

Rage addicts can easily snap over the perception that they are either late or falling behind. Almost always, they blame this on others and take it out on them. One of the quickest ways to learn patience is to practice recovery driving. We learned about this in chapter one. It starts by being willing to move over into the right hand lane and drive 5 miles per hour *under* the speed limit. Learning to accept this limit on your attempt to control your life through speeding will easily translate into patience in other areas, too. Practicing patience is one of the quickest ways to get your wife's attention and to regain her trust.

10. Practice forgiveness – not punishment.

Perhaps the easiest way to understand forgiveness is to first look at unforgiveness. Unforgiveness is basically the sense of being "owed" – an apology, restitution of some sort, reinstatement of some position lost, etc. In unforgiveness, you resolve to stay angry at someone – reminding yourself almost every day of the way that person failed me or hurt me – until that person comes and fixes what has been ruined. Meanwhile, they are off in Hawaii on a 3-month vacation and couldn't care less! Unforgiveness – and the anger it produces – is the poison you swallow yourself in your attempt to get back at someone else. Forgiveness is the act of letting go of that debt by surrendering to the conviction that whatever someone else took from you does not have the power to stop God from bringing you to a place in life that is safe, successful and good. Quit taking the poison and let those old debts go.

Forgive us our debts, as we forgive our debtors. (Luke 11:4)

This issue is too important to leave just yet. Choosing to forgive is a major step in recovery from any addictive behavior. It is one thing to read about the value of forgiveness, but reading about it and agreeing that it is a good idea are not the same as actually doing it. There is no time like the present for putting this principle into practice. In the space below, make a list of all the people that you feel have harmed you in some way that has left you still angry. Maybe you actually have thoughts of revenge; or maybe you are only still holding on to the delusion that they should come back and fix what they broke and make everything all better again. If you are staying angry and waiting for something to happen, you need to forgive. You need to let go of the debt. So write their names on the next page, along with a very brief description of the offense they committed against you:

For example:

    My dad   *He always made fun of my speech impediment.*

    My boss   *He gave Kevin the promotion I deserved.*

NAME   **OFFENSE**

_____

_____

_____

_____

_____

_____

_____

_____

_____

_____

_____

_____

_____

_____

_____

_____

_____

_____

Now go back and turn this list into a prayer list, releasing to God the debt that you feel each of these people still owes you. If the idea of praying is new to you, just know there aren't any real rules. Just tell God how you feel and what you want to happen here.

For example: *God, today I am releasing my dad from the debt of apologizing to me for how he made fun of me. (It is important to pray this prayer, even if your dad has passed away).*

Now, find a quiet spot where you won't be interrupted and take all the time you need to simply talk to God about everyone on this list.

When you are done with the whole list, close out this time by praying a prayer similar to this

God, I am through living my life as a reaction to what other people have done to me. I am through using their offenses as an excuse for my offenses. I am trusting You to bring me to a place in life that is safe, successful and good, in spite of what they might have taken from me. Help me every day to release old debts, and to not collect new ones, either. – Amen

_____   _____

Signed   Date

11. Practice losing – not winning.

If you are one of those guys who needs to win — which you define as "being right" — at all costs, things are almost certain to turn out wrong. First of all, since you are not God, you are very often going to be wrong, whether you believe it or not. Second of all, pressing your side until you "win" an argument, with your wife for example, is going to wound her deeply. To gain the respect and trust of your wife, be ready and willing to lose. Most of the time winning is just not worth it.

12. Practice being wrong – not right.

This is very closely related to the previous principle. In addition to being willing to lose, start being willing to let others be right. Don't place so much value in having your opinions or plans acknowledged as superior to everyone else's. Your position may not technically be wrong, but pushing your opinions on others – especially your wife – is very often a wrong idea. Contrary to what you want to believe, there is usually more than one way to do a right thing. It won't kill you to let her be right. It may kill your marriage if you don't.

13. Practice humility – not self-righteousness.

This principle is at the heart of all we are trying to achieve in this chapter. Once you understand what humility really is you will spend the rest of your life pursuing it, but in the process you will bring much more good into the lives of others. Some people think that humility is kind of like groveling in the dust – putting yourself down in front of others. But humility is simply the art of *raising other people up* and treating them in a way that makes it clear that you think they are just as important and just as valuable as yourself.

Self-righteousness uses anger to control and put other people down, justifying this unkind behavior on the basis of the "love" that is behind it. Just remember, you can't practice humility or love by humiliating people.

14. Practice being compassionate – not angry at injustice toward others.

Rageaholics are convinced that they must hold on to their anger because they might need it some day in order to fight for a just cause. Just ask yourself this question: When was the last time flying into a rage really helped you or your family? Very often this will take a bad situation and turn it into a genuine tragedy.

Nothing helps heal relationships and solves problems faster or better than showing a little compassion. Tim Sanders, in his best-selling book, *Love is the Killer App*, says it like this: "People are hungry for compassion. There's never enough of it. And the tougher the times are, the more important it becomes."

The Japanese martial arts discipline known as Aikido teaches how to throw and grapple with an opponent. But above all, it teaches how to work for reconciliation and conflict resolution. An Aikido master who resorts to physical violence believes he has already lost the most important battle. Try thinking more along those lines. Look for ways to resolve conflict that do not involve expressing anger. Listen and learn to understand your spouse's needs and worries. Reach out to her with love instead of retaliation. You will both be winners.

15. Practice being persistent in dealing with your anger – not, "How much more do you want me to take?"

In Episode 5 of the Star Wars saga, *The Empire Strikes Back*, Luke Skywalker is hurrying to complete his training to become a Jedi master. All he has to do is retrieve his fighter ship that crashed and is now buried in a swamp. And all he is allowed to use is the psycho-kinetic power of the Force. He protests to his trainer, Master Yoda, that it is too hard. Finally he agrees to at least try, to which Yoda responds, "Do or do not do. There is no try!"

Recovering from anger addiction is hard. No one ever said it would be easy. All we said is that it would be worth it. Some days will go much better than others. Some days you will just want to quit altogether, letting yourself off the hook by saying that at least you "tried." Our encouragement to you is to get past the idea that you are only obligated to do the minimum. Stay at it. Don't just commit to try; *commit to get the job done*. Have we already mentioned that if you don't quit, you can't lose? We really mean it.

16. Practice understanding – not explaining.

Anger addicts waste a lot of time trying to explain and justify their incredibly destructive, inappropriate actions. There is hardly ever a good reason for trampling on the feelings of those who love you or for treating them with disrespect. Explaining only deepens the wounds and stokes your own anger fires. Instead of explaining, try listening and learning. Try to find out what fears or needs or dreams are motivating your wife. Once you understand her well enough to accurately explain these things back to her, your anger will need no explanation because it will have gone stone cold.

17. Practice feeling awkward – not feeling natural.

Angry men who start practicing the principles in this book regularly report feeling very unnatural and strange. You will too, for a while. When will you be able to get back to feeling like yourself? Hopefully, never! Being yourself is what got you into trouble in the first place! Integrating these new skills and principles into your everyday life is going to take patience and practice. And it will take time. So get used to feeling awkward. It is a definite sign of progress!

18. Practice balancing your life – not careerism.

Ragers cannot work 80 hours a week and expect to overcome their addiction, must less stay married. You have to have relaxation and rest if you want to make progress in your recovery. Devote more time to hiking, napping, singing, reading great books, playing with the kids or grandkids, going for rides in the country with your wife (at 5 miles below the speed limit). Spend less time on the job. Stop worrying about the job. Work will still be there Monday morning. Can you say the same for your family?

Before we leave this principle, let's take a quick time allotment inventory. In the spaces below, estimate the percentage of your time every week that is devoted to the following activities. Remember, it has to add up to 100%.

ACTIVITY	PERCENTAGE OF TIME PER WEEK
Work-related, income producing	_____
Sleeping	_____
Watching TV, nighttime channel surfing	_____
Undistracted, positive interaction with wife	_____
Undistracted, positive interaction with kids	_____
Exercise and fitness workout	_____
Hobbies and leisure	_____
Self-improvement	_____
Meals	_____
Socializing with friends (guys only)	_____
Socializing with friends (couples)	_____
Surfing the Internet	_____
Spiritual disciplines like prayer, meditation or study	_____
Other (list below)	
_____	_____
_____	_____
TOTAL	_____

Does this total 100%?

It is very difficult to come up with an activity list that is totally comprehensive, because everyone's lifestyle is different. What we are really looking for here is an answer to the question, "Is my life well-balanced?" Look for percentages that are completely unreasonable and out of line. Where would it be a good idea to cut back? What activities need to be given a higher priority?

The most important thing you can do – as always – is to show this list to your wife. Does she agree with the percentages you have written here? What are the areas she would like for you to adjust? Give some serious thought to her requests, and ask yourself what it would take to make changes in those areas.

19. PRACTICE STAYING ON THE PATH – NOT CURSING YOUR LUCK.

It is said that the most common entry in Christopher Columbus' logbook is simply, "Today, we sailed on." Imagine that, day after day of nothing but empty horizons. Were they headed in the right direction? Were they going to fall off the edge of the earth? Were they going to hit the jackpot at the end of the journey? On most days, there was simply no way to tell. It was too late to turn back. They just sailed on.

Recovery from anger addiction is a process, not an event. It is day after day of sailing on, staying true to the plan, correcting your course, learning from your mistakes, pressing on towards healthier belief systems, better attitudes, wiser choices and deeper relationships. It is a journey that truly has no end. But it can become more pleasant and satisfying with each new day and each new victory. Oh, and remember: if you don't quit, you can't lose.

20. PRACTICE DAILY SPIRITUAL MEDITATION – NOT SLEEPING LATE.

Earlier we mentioned that spirituality is simply being open to the possibility of God touching your life. You will increase your chances of that actually happening if you make time during your day to *allow God an opportunity* to touch you. The simplest thing to do is to set aside maybe as few as 10 or 15 minutes in quiet meditation. All religious traditions value this kind of experience for clearing the mind, relaxing the body and tuning up the spirit. Find a place that is still and peaceful. Sit down in a comfortable position. Close your eyes and try to simply focus on the sound of your breathing. Breathe deeply and slowly – inhale for 3 seconds, hold it for 3 seconds, then exhale for three seconds. Focus on the rhythm as well as the sound. Continue this breathing cycle until you are feeling peaceful and relaxed. Allow your mind to be aware of your feelings, but don't try to analyze them or find any solutions to your problems. Instead, simply ask God to guide you, to heal you, to take control. If you have a specific need, don't be afraid to pray a specific prayer. But then release it all into His control – don't spend any time trying to figure out what you have to do to get the prayer answered. Stay in this relaxed state as long time will allow. And take a note pad with you. Very often, meditation allows your inner self to "hear" insights that will be helpful to you when you have to return to the noisy outside world.

*"Today, I gave myself 15 minutes of quiet time to meditate. It was a simple, peaceful time — a spiritually refreshing time. I look forward to doing it again **every day** this week. The best time of day for me to commune with God is _____."*

_____   _____
               Signature   Date

ASSESS *Your Spiritual Values*

Now that we have a glimpse at what a life well grounded in spiritual values might look like, let's get an honest assessment of what your life looks like. Below is the list of 20 spiritual principles that we have been discussing. Study the list carefully; go back over the summary of any principle that you aren't clear on. Then begin by assessing how often you feel that you demonstrate each quality in your life by putting a circle around the letter that best describes your behavior pattern, with

> A = Always
> O = Often
> S = Sometimes
> R = Rarely
> N = Never

Then go over the list one final time, placing a check mark (✓) next to the five principles you feel you are strongest in, and a minus (–) next to the five principles you feel need the most work or the most immediate attention.

Spiritual Self-Assessment — Rating by Me

Spiritual Principle	I practice this principle:
✓ –	
☐ ☐ Self-restraint	A O S R N
☐ ☐ Kindness	A O S R N
☐ ☐ Graciousness	A O S R N
☐ ☐ Self-examination	A O S R N
☐ ☐ Empathy	A O S R N
☐ ☐ Surrender	A O S R N
☐ ☐ Service to Others	A O S R N
☐ ☐ Self-discipline	A O S R N
☐ ☐ Patience	A O S R N
☐ ☐ Forgiveness	A O S R N
☐ ☐ Willingness to lose instead of win	A O S R N
☐ ☐ Willingness to be wrong instead of right	A O S R N
☐ ☐ Humility	A O S R N
☐ ☐ Compassion	A O S R N
☐ ☐ Persistence in dealing with my anger	A O S R N
☐ ☐ Willingness to understand others, not explain myself	A O S R N
☐ ☐ Willingness to feel awkward	A O S R N
☐ ☐ Balance in my life	A O S R N
☐ ☐ Success in staying on the path	A O S R N
☐ ☐ Daily spiritual meditation	A O S R N

Next, just as in the previous chapter, your spouse or accountability partner should have an opportunity here to provide a second opinion. Remember, we are not questioning your integrity, just your memory. In addition, your behavior may affect your wife in a way that you don't understand. We have reprinted the list below, so that she can provide both her assessment of how often you practice this principle and her suggestion for which ones need the most immediate work. Ask her to circle the letter that best describes how frequently she sees you demonstrating each principle in your life. Give her a chance to study the summary in the previous pages if she needs to. Finally, ask her to place a check (√) in front of the five items that she thinks you are strongest in and to place a minus (—) next to the five that need the most work or require the most immediate attention.

Spiritual Self-Assessment — Rating by My Spouse

Spiritual Principle	I practice this principle:
✓ –	
☐ ☐ Self-restraint	A O S R N
☐ ☐ Kindness	A O S R N
☐ ☐ Graciousness	A O S R N
☐ ☐ Self-examination	A O S R N
☐ ☐ Empathy	A O S R N
☐ ☐ Surrender	A O S R N
☐ ☐ Service to Others	A O S R N
☐ ☐ Self-discipline	A O S R N
☐ ☐ Patience	A O S R N
☐ ☐ Forgiveness	A O S R N
☐ ☐ Willingness to lose instead of win	A O S R N
☐ ☐ Willingness to be wrong instead of right	A O S R N
☐ ☐ Humility	A O S R N
☐ ☐ Compassion	A O S R N
☐ ☐ Persistence in dealing with my anger	A O S R N
☐ ☐ Willingness to understand others, not explain myself	A O S R N
☐ ☐ Willingness to feel awkward	A O S R N
☐ ☐ Balance in my life	A O S R N
☐ ☐ Success in staying on the path	A O S R N
☐ ☐ Daily spiritual meditation	A O S R N

Now, compare your assessment with your wife's assessment. Did each of you come up with about the same results? It would be a good sign if you did, but it would also be a big surprise! Most of the time anger addicts minimize their failures and maximize what they think their strong points are. We rarely have any idea of how our behavior is affecting those around us, and we are clueless about what they may be really wishing we would work on the most. So, if you and your wife agree on the results, GREAT! Otherwise, take her scores and move on to the next exercise.

List below the five principles that need the most work or the most immediate attention.

_____

_____

_____

_____

Break through *to a richer life*

Just as in the previous chapter, the first step in learning how to grow in these important principles is to take a moment to study recent examples where you have failed to follow them. Begin by summarizing a recent event or behavior pattern, one for each of the principles identified above, giving evidence that you failed to apply it in that situation and stating the results.

For example:

Principle not followed: *Willing to be wrong instead of right.*

When: *Tuesday night after dinner.*

Where: *In the family room.*

Who was involved: *Just my wife – Kate – and me.*

What happened: *We were watching a movie on TV and she mentioned that she really liked one of the actors and especially liked the character he played in a movie that came out about 5 years ago. I was pretty sure that she was wrong, so I told her so. I not only told her that she was mistaken, I told her who the main actor was in that movie, a guy that I don't like at all. And I told her it was a dumb movie. She argued for a minute but I just kept feeding her more details from the movie and finally she just kept quiet. We didn't talk much, or do anything else for that matter – if you know what I mean, for the rest of the night.*

Now use this example to help you replay examples of the way you failed to apply each of the principles on your list. If you can't think of an example for one of the principles, ask your wife. She may be able to give you several examples.

Principle not followed: _____

When: _____

Where: _____

Who was involved: _____

_____

What happened: _____

_____

_____

_____

_____
_____
_____

PRINCIPLE NOT FOLLOWED: _____

When: _____

Where: _____

Who was involved: _____
_____

What happened: _____
_____
_____
_____
_____
_____
_____

PRINCIPLE NOT FOLLOWED: _____

When: _____

Where: _____

Who was involved: _____
_____

What happened: _____
_____
_____
_____
_____

_____

_____

Principle not followed: _____

When: _____

Where: _____

Who was involved: _____

_____

What happened: _____

_____

_____

_____

_____

_____

_____

Principle not followed: _____

When: _____

Where: _____

Who was involved: _____

_____

What happened: _____

_____

_____

_____

_____

_____

Principle not followed: _____

When: _____

Where: _____

Who was involved: _____
_____

What happened: _____
_____
_____
_____
_____
_____
_____

Now that you have a pretty good idea of what happened, maybe it would be good to ask, "Why?" What was going through your mind that was pushing you to make an unhealthy or hurtful choice? Do you suppose you could recall what it is you were feeling or believing that was pushing your button during that event?

Let's go back to our example on page 86. What do you suppose was up with Kate's husband? We can only guess, but it might have been something like this:

Principle not followed: *Willing to be wrong instead of right.*

Underlying feelings or beliefs: *Need to feel superior, need to impress her with how much he knew, tired of her talking about that particular actor – maybe feeling a little jealous or insecure thinking she might be comparing him to that actor.*

We will never know for sure about Kate's husband, but you ought to have some clue about what was going on inside of you during each of those five events. In the spaces below, briefly summarize what you were feeling or believing during the event.

Principle not followed: _____

Underlying feelings or belief: _____
_____

_____

Principle not followed: _____

Underlying feelings or belief: _____

_____

_____

Principle not followed: _____

Underlying feelings or belief: _____

_____

_____

Principle not followed: _____

Underlying feelings or belief: _____

_____

_____

Principle not followed: _____

Underlying feelings or belief: _____

_____

_____

Principle not followed: _____

Underlying feelings or belief: _____

_____

_____

Chapter 2 • Check-Up from the Neck Up

LET'S MAKE A NEW MOVIE.

Now, it is time to go back and rewrite the script. What do suppose might have happened if you had been able or willing to apply the appropriate spiritual principle to that situation?

Let's revisit our example on page 86. Kate's husband just wanted to be right. What if he had been willing to be wrong, or, more clearly stated, what if he had been willing for Kate to express her opinion without being compelled to point out that she was wrong?

PRINCIPLE NOT FOLLOWED: *Willing to be wrong instead of right.*

Instead of saying or thinking the things that he did, Kate's husband could have: *simply told myself that it was no big deal. Really, who cares whether this actor was in that movie or not? Is it worth starting an argument over and hurting her feelings? What if I just said, "you may be right," and we just went on watching the movie and having a nice evening? Sounds pretty good to me.*

Now, go back and rescript your five examples by describing things you could have thought or done that would have helped the event to have a happier ending.

PRINCIPLE NOT FOLLOWED: _____

Instead of saying or thinking the things that I did, I could have: _____

_____
_____
_____
_____
_____

PRINCIPLE NOT FOLLOWED: _____

Instead of saying or thinking the things that I did, I could have: _____

_____
_____
_____

_____
_____

Principle not followed: _____

Instead of saying or thinking the things that I did, I could have: _____
_____
_____
_____
_____
_____

Principle not followed: _____

Instead of saying or thinking the things that I did, I could have: _____
_____
_____
_____
_____
_____

Principle not followed: _____

Instead of saying or thinking the things that I did, I could have: _____
_____
_____
_____

_____
_____

PRINCIPLE NOT FOLLOWED: _____

Instead of saying or thinking the things that I did, I could have: _____

_____
_____
_____
_____
_____

Learning to see with new eyes

One of the most important benefits of spiritual growth is that you will begin to be aware that you are surrounded by opportunities to think and act differently than you did before. Remember the line from that famous old hymn, *Amazing Grace* – "[I] Was blind but now I see"? One of the main reasons for this chapter is to help you learn to see with new eyes so that you can make new, healthier, happier choices. You are **not** a slave to your anger! You can change what you believe and how you act.

Of course, hindsight is always 20-20. It is easy to look back now, using the information that we have shared with you here, and see what you could have done differently. But life doesn't work that way, does it? Life requires us to make quick decisions; seemingly innocent, almost random events can take us by surprise and anger can boil over before we even realize it. Over 150 years ago, famous French chemist and microbiologist Louis Pasteur observed that, *"chance favors the prepared mind."* This simply means that, while we don't control when or how things happen, we can prepare in advance to make the best of every situation that hits us. Remember the Boy Scout motto: Be Prepared!

So let's take one more run at these five principles that we have been working on for the last few pages. Take a few minutes to envision a scenario – preferably one that you could reasonably expect to encounter on a typical day – that would require you to be ready to follow one of the five principles we have been discussing. Start by describing the place where it might occur and the people who might be involved. Then describe the nature of the situation, and why it will require you to follow this particular principle. The last step is to write out in detail what you would tell yourself in that situation, based on the principle you are trying to learn, and then describe the course of action you would choose, based on that same principle.

Principle to follow: _____

Place it might occur: _____

Persons involved: _____

Nature of the situation, including why it would require me to follow this particular principle: _____
_____
_____
_____
_____

What I will tell myself the next time I face this situation: _____
_____
_____
_____
_____

Course of action I will follow, based on this principle: _____
_____
_____
_____
_____
_____

Principle to follow: _____

Place it might occur: _____

Persons involved: _____

Nature of the situation, including why it would require me to follow this particular principle: _____
_____
_____

Chapter 2 • *Check-Up from the Neck Up*

_____

_____

What I will tell myself the next time I face this situation: _____

_____

_____

_____

_____

Course of action I will follow, based on this principle: _____

_____

_____

_____

_____

PRINCIPLE TO FOLLOW: _____

Place it might occur: _____

Persons involved: _____

Nature of the situation, including why it would require me to follow this particular principle: _____

_____

_____

_____

What I will tell myself the next time I face this situation: _____

_____

_____

_____

Course of action I will follow, based on this principle: _____
_____
_____
_____
_____

PRINCIPLE TO FOLLOW: _____

Place it might occur: _____

Persons involved: _____

Nature of the situation, including why it would require me to follow this particular principle: _____
_____
_____
_____
_____

What I will tell myself the next time I face this situation: _____
_____
_____
_____
_____

Course of action I will follow, based on this principle: _____
_____
_____
_____
_____

PRINCIPLE TO FOLLOW: _____

Place it might occur: _____

Persons involved: _____

Nature of the situation, including why it would require me to follow this particular principle: _____

_____

_____

_____

_____

What I will tell myself the next time I face this situation: _____

_____

_____

_____

_____

Course of action I will follow, based on this principle: _____

_____

_____

_____

_____

One final note on the process we have been working on here. It is likely that you may have more than five principles that you need to practice. After you have completed all the work in this chapter devoted to the five principles that needed the most attention, it is a simple matter to repeat these exercises for any other principles that also need attention. If you aren't sure if there are any other areas, ask your wife if she has any input.

Chart Your Progress

The final stage in learning to apply these new principles is to develop a system to measure your progress. You are already using the charts from chapter one to document your progress for abstaining from angry behaviors. Instead of adding one more big chart to keep up with, this time we will use note cards. Take five 3x5 or 4x6 cards, readily available at any local drug store, and write one of the five high-priority principles you have been working on in this chapter one the front of each card. If the card is blank on one side and has lines on the other side, write the name of the principle on the blank side. Keep these cards with you at all times, and before every meal, take them out and simply read and speak each of these principles to yourself. As you go over each one, remind yourself of the scenarios we have discussed in this chapter. Review the plans you have made for applying these principles whenever the need arises.

On the back of the card — the side with the lines — record your progress on each principle at the end of every day. Write the date and then give yourself a grade.

> A = successful application of the principle each time it was needed today
> B = it was a little shaky, but stuck to the script every time it was needed today
> C = didn't do all that great, definitely missed a chance, hopefully no real damage
> D and F = outright disaster, totally blew it, in the doghouse big time

For any situation that got a grade of C or lower, assess what happened by going back and reconstructing the events using the guidelines you learned from this chapter. After rethinking what happened and how you could have responded better, write a scenario describing how you will handle the situation differently next time. As always, let your wife in on this process, especially if she was involved in any of the situations, and use her input to create the most accurate grade for each principle and event.

Seeing with new eyes, practicing new life principles, takes practice. You have already come so far. Don't let failures discourage you. Just learn from them and be better prepared next time. You are well on your way to controlling your anger addiction.

CHAPTER 3
Put a Sock In It

Did you ever see that public service TV commercial produced by the Partnership for a Drug Free America that showed eggs frying in a skillet, with voice-over announcing, "this is your brain on drugs"? The advertising industry has declared this ad campaign to be one of the most influential commercials of all time. And why is that? Because it really is true that a picture is worth a thousand words. Well, picture this:

Carter, 46, and Rachel, 42, have made plans to meet friends for dinner at a very nice restaurant this evening. It is supposed to be a celebration of Rachel's promotion at work. She hurries home, spends over an hour bathing and doing her hair and make-up. She has bought an elegant new dress to wear for this special occasion. She is looking forward to the evening.

Meanwhile, Carter is late ... again. Rachel is practically dressed when he walks through the front door. Their reservation is for less than an hour from now, and Carter is clearly not moving fast enough to get them all the way downtown in time to meet their friends. He is still trying to decide what to wear, and mulling over whether or not to take a shower.

Frustrated, Rachel urges him to please hurry. Carter responds that he has been hurrying all day and is not at all inclined to bust his "rear-end" just so they can be on time for a dinner date. At that point, Rachel, in a tone that is unmistakable for its disappointment and anger, replies, "Well, you wouldn't have to be busting your 'rear-end' if you had tried harder to get here on time. You knew this night was special to me. Why couldn't you have made it a priority just this once to put work second and me first? Why didn't you plan to leave work on time? Or would it have killed you to even get off a little early just this once?"

What you have read so far is just the set-up, kind of like the beginning of the drug commercial where they start out by saying "This is your brain" ... (before they say, "and this is your brain on drugs"). Got the picture so far? *"This is Carter ..."* Now, up next is either *"... and this is Carter either making a colossal mistake"* or *"... and this is Carter pulling out a remarkable save."*

You are now going to read two possible endings for the story above. In a way, it is kind of like being part of one of those test audiences for a movie that is about to be released. Your job now is to pick the ending that has the best possible chance of getting Carter out of the doghouse and maybe even saving his marriage. Back to the story.

ENDING NUMBER ONE:

"Look, Rachel," Carter snaps. "I had important things to do today, too. You aren't the only one who has a big important job with a big important company. My company counts on me to give them 100% and that's what I do. I can't afford to cut and run for every little tea party that you plan for you and your little friends. We can get there late, or we can forget the whole thing. Now get out of my face and let me decide if am going to take a shower or just sit here and rest a minute!"

ENDING NUMBER TWO:

Carter catches himself, takes a deep breath and says, "I'm so sorry, Rachel. Can you ever forgive me for being so insensitive and selfish? I don't know what got into me just now. I must be crazy or stupid or both to come so close to ruining your special evening. Let me just splash some water on my face and change shirts. I'll be ready to go in five minutes."

Even without seeing this live, we hope you still get the picture. If you voted for ending number one, then you need to go back and redo the first two chapters of this book! This is a no-brainer slam-dunk. If Carter picks ending number one, he is deep in the doghouse, sleeping on the couch tonight and probably well on his way to sleeping alone permanently—at least as far as Rachel is concerned.

On the other hand, if he is smart enough, quick enough and sincere enough to correct his trajectory in mid-sentence and go for ending number two, he is probably out of the deep doghouse, maybe even out of the doghouse altogether. If he can build on this momentum for the rest of the evening, by the time they get home, Rachel may even forget this unpleasant event ever happened. And that could be a good thing, too.

So, who in his right mind would ever choose anything else except ending number two, or some variation of it, whenever he has done something hurtful or offensive to his wife? Anger addicts, of course. They choose the wrong answer all the time, often more than once in the same day – sometimes more than once in the same sentence! The goal of this chapter is to help you begin to change this pattern, and learn to communicate with your wife in a way that is helpful instead of hurtful.

START BY PUTTING A SOCK IN IT

By now you have already been practicing abstaining from talking when you are angry. The less you talk, the less likely you are to say the kind of stupid things that could have (maybe they did?) landed Carter in trouble. Shutting up – or putting a sock it – and walking away is always a good strategy.

But sometimes you just can't get away with saying nothing. You are in the doghouse and you have to be accountable for your behavior over something that has wounded your wife in a very real and deep way. Take note here: shutting up and walking away may not work – it may even make things worse. In a situation like this, "putting a sock in it" doesn't mean saying nothing, *it means not saying what you would normally say, what you would like to say, and instead saying something that would really help resolve the situation.*

WHEN YOU FIND YOURSELF IN THE DOGHOUSE, DON'T KEEPING ACTING LIKE A DOG

A lot of the information found in this chapter can be very helpful even to men who aren't rageaholics. But anger addicts create – or at least escalate – many arguments and conflicts with their angry responses. For men like this, the principles discussed here can literally be the *love-saver* you have been looking for.

First of all, we need to make a distinction between two kinds of situations that anger addicts create with their wives. We call them the *deep doghouse* and the *shallow doghouse*. Neither situation is good, but being in the deep doghouse definitely calls for more drastic and immediate action. Let's look at this one first.

BEING IN THE DEEP DOGHOUSE

You know you are in the deep doghouse when your wife is overtly, extremely angry with you. Her tone is harsh, her words are critical, and she rarely communicates anything to you except extreme displeasure, open hostility and maybe even serious threats of divorce. Very often, waking up in the deep doghouse is what finally pushes an anger addict to go to a therapist or other helping professional. He has finally run out of tricks, trinkets, promises and, most significantly, the ability to intimidate and control with anger. He is now ready to ask for help.

Maybe that is how you ended up reading this book. Maybe you have even started to learn to control your anger by abstaining from the destructive behaviors we noted earlier. Maybe you are even trying to be more open to "spiritual stuff." And maybe you are *still in the deep doghouse* with your wife. She is still angry with you; she is still barely talking to you. You still aren't allowed back into the house, and she thinks that the changes you are starting to make are just one more trick to weasel your way back into a relationship that she is ready to flush.

If this sounds familiar, then may we make a suggestion? Move these three little words to the very top of your conversation list *immediately*:

"You Are Right."

The vast majority of anger addicts get into discussions that lead to arguments that lead to very noisy fights that sometimes lead to trips downtown in a squad car because they are *unwilling to lose*. It is just a guy thing to defend yourself, to protect your territory and justify your actions. It is important to a guy's sense of "guy-ness" to believe he is right about practically everything. You are not God. This can only lead to one obvious conclusion: Sometimes – maybe a lot of the time – *you are going to be at least a little bit wrong*, and **maybe extremely wrong**. But you are a guy so you just keep defending yourself to your wife. And the more you defend yourself, the wronger and wronger you get. And your wife begins to think you are a jerk, because you are acting like a jerk. She decides you don't really care about her or her needs and feelings. (That would be because you are sending a clear message that you only care about yourself.) And if this goes on long enough, she decides she doesn't really love you and she doesn't trust you. If you want to nip this whole thing in the bud, just learn to lose by learning to say, "You are right."

Now, on those rare occasions where you might even be completely justified in the opinion you have expressed, are we asking you to go ahead and lie? Well, kinda, but not exactly. Remember, arguments are no good for anger addicts. They will *always* lead you in the wrong direction by turning up the fire under your pressure cooker. So we want to suggest a way for you to cool that fire and maintain a loving communication connection with your wife. If you are in the deep doghouse – or headed in that direction – use this strategy to head off an argument:

1. *Say the phrase, "You are right."*

2. *Find some grain of truth in what she is saying, and agree with that.*

3. *Get your "but" out of the way. Don't say, "You are right, but …"*

Don't argue, don't defend, don't explain, don't justify, don't preach, don't utter any other words other than "You are right." Find some way to agree with her and defuse the conversation as fast as you can. You may have an opportunity to express your opinion later (much later) when you are for sure out of the deep doghouse.

THE CBSSW PHRASES

Very often, your wife may be surprised or suspicious when you suddenly agree with her. She may ask you a few more questions, just to try to nail down what is really going on. If that happens, rely on the CBSSW phrases. These letters stand for

CRAZY

BAD

STUPID

SICK

WRONG

Insert these words into whatever response you make to her questions, as follows:

"It was a totally crazy reaction. I don't know what's wrong with me."

"That was just bad and stupid of me."

"I was stupid to have done (or said or thought) that."

"I was wrong. You were right."

"I must be really sick to even think like that."

You can even combine them, if needed, for serious deep doghouse conversations:

"I was completely crazy to say that. You are absolutely right; it was a very bad thing I did."

The point here is to avoid an argument at all costs, or at least stop the argument from getting any worse. It is not worth risking your marriage just for the privilege of getting in the last word.

Write these phrases on a 3x5 card and carry them in your pocket. Review them at least 3 times a day. Do this for two straight weeks.

Putting an End to Marital Tug-of-War

We have alluded to this principle previously, but let's review it one more time right here, just so there is no mistake. Tug-of-war games are fun at picnics and youth summer camps, but they are deadly for marriages. Trying to drag your spouse through the mud and over to your side only leads to rope burns, hurt feelings and broken trust. Flexing your anger muscles and flaunting your machismo during an argument with your wife is not romantic or attractive. It **hurts**. And it will get you into the deep doghouse. If you want to beat your addiction and protect your marriage, *let go of your end of the rope* any time you sense a conflict may be developing. And do it as kindly and cheerfully as you can. It takes two sides to make a tug-of-war, *but only one side to end it*. Don't be afraid to let go of your end of the rope. It takes a lot of courage and strength to do it. But isn't courage and strength what it takes to be a manly man in the first place? Just let it go a few times and see what happens.

Shallow Doghouse Communication

The difference between shallow doghouse communication and deep doghouse communication is that in shallow doghouse communication your wife may actually be speaking to you without yelling, attacking or threatening to leave. However, if it is still obvious that she is upset with you – cold, withdrawn, not receptive to physical contact – then you are at least still in the shallow doghouse. Now it may be time to apologize and try to make amends for the wounds you have caused. Use these phrases to start the conversation, especially if you are both clear on why she is angry with you and what you have done to hurt her:

"I AM REALLY SORRY."

"IT WAS ALL MY FAULT."

"PLEASE FORGIVE ME."

WHAT CAN I DO TO MAKE IT UP TO YOU?"

You can even mix some of the CBSSW phrases to emphasize your desire to take responsibility for your actions. For instance:

"Honey, I am really sorry I yelled at you in the car on the way home yesterday. It was wrong of me. I must be crazy to talk to you like that. It was all my fault. Please forgive me."

WARNING! WARNING!

DANGER! DANGER!

DO NOT — REPEAT — DO NOT TRY TO APOLOGIZE TO YOUR WIFE USING ANY VERSION OF THIS PHRASE:

"I am sorry IF what I did or said upset you or hurt your feelings."

There are no *ifs, ands* or *buts* about it. If she is acting upset or hurt or angry, it is because **she is**. And it is **because of what you did.** Trying to slip by her with a conditional semi-apology is a huge insult and a sure one-way ticket back to the deep doghouse. It is actually a way of putting her down by implying that she shouldn't have been hurt by what you did but, oh well, if she was then you are certainly man enough to apologize. Listen carefully and you can probably already hear her saying:

*"IF? What do you mean, IF? Were we even in the same car yesterday? Do you remember what you said to me? How could you possibly **not** think I was upset because of what you did?!"*

If you are dumb enough or insensitive enough to pull a stunt like this, your only hope is to immediately fall back on the CBSSW phrases and hope for the best. And make sure there are sheets on the hide-a-bed.

ONE MORE IMPORTANT PHRASE

In a lot of ways, this final phrase in the shallow doghouse vocabulary may be the most important. Apologies can seem pretty empty after you have offered them over and over again for years without ever demonstrating any real change in your attitude. So if you really want your wife to believe that you want to change and that you are working on changing, the first step in the right direction may be to say this:

"What can I do to make it up to you?"

Don't offer to do something that you THINK might make it up to her; no more gifts or flowers or other peace offerings as you have tried in the past. Instead, *let her choose.* This is really important. How will she know that you are truly willing to change unless you are willing to quit controlling her, even during the "make-up" phase of your anger cycle? So after you have *sincerely* apologized to her in every way you can think of, ask her, *"What can I do to make it up to you?"* And then let *her* choose.

Be prepared for the fact that she may still give you the cold shoulder at first, because she assumes that this is just another one of your games. Don't pressure her, but every couple of days just politely tell her again, *"I am really serious. I am really sorry. What can I do to make it up to you?"*

Oh, and one more thing. Eventually she will probably tell you something you can do that would help her to get over her anger and trust you more. Whatever it is, just **do it!** Be enthusiastic. Smile. Do it as fast and as well as you can. Don't complain or argue or try to make a deal. Just do it. Whatever it may cost you in terms of time, money, pride or inconvenience will definitely more than pay for itself in the long run. You may not only get out of the doghouse, but you may also get your marriage back.

Assess Your Doghouse Communication Skills

So, now you have some understanding of what it means to be in the doghouse, and what to do to get out, depending on whether you are in the "deep" doghouse or the "shallow" doghouse. What we don't know yet is the pattern you typically follow when you are in the doghouse. Begin by thinking back on two recent arguments that landed you in a deep doghouse situation. Your wife was very angry, yelling, criticizing, accusing – maybe even threatening to call the police or file for divorce. Maybe she did call the police or file for divorce. Yeah, it was that kind of an argument.

What we need to know now is what it was about, what you said, and what happened as a result of what you said.

For example:

Louise and Richard were arguing again about whether or not to get a new car. Their budget was tight, but their car was getting old. As a matter of fact, the alternator gave out and left her stranded at the mall last week. She had to wait an hour for Richard to get home from a late sales call and come and pick her up. The conversation went something like this:

> Louise: *Richard, can't we please do something about getting another car? Every time I ask you, there is always some excuse. And in the meantime, I never know when I am going to get stranded someplace in the dark of night. I don't feel safe and I don't know how many more surprises I can take.*

Richard: Look, Louise. You know good and well that the reason we can't afford a car is because you ran up all that credit card debt last year to start your whacky Internet business that made us exactly twelve dollars and thirty-four cents! I am sick of your whining about the car, I am sick of you whining period. You just worry about fixing me some supper and let me worry about the *&#!$ car!

Two days later, while Richard was away on a weekend fishing trip with his brother, Louise packed a suitcase, put it in Richard's pick-up (he left it at home and went in his brother's truck), and went to stay with a friend in the next county. It took Richard almost a week to figure out were she was.

That story had a lot of information in it; more than we really need for this exercise. But we gave you the whole picture so you could see how we are going to shrink it down to the basics. We will now show you how to reduce this story down to a few key details, so you will know how to describe your own deep doghouse arguments. We don't expect you to reconstruct anything word for word, like we did above. That is why we are going to translate Richard and Louise's argument into "argument shorthand" and enter it below.

Argument One

Persons involved: *Just Richard and Louise.*

Reason for disagreement: *Car is old and Louise wanted to get a new one.*

What she said: *Basically, she just said that she wasn't happy driving an old car around that might break on her somewhere and leave her stranded again, and she wanted to talk about getting another one.*

What he said: *He blamed the whole problem on her foolish business venture last year, told her to shut up and get him something to eat, and used profanity to emphasize how angry he was at her for bringing it up.*

Deep Doghouse result: *She took his truck and left him.*

Do you see how this works? We didn't really need to have the word-for-word account of the argument to get a pretty good idea about what happened. We just need to know the basics: who was involved, the reason for the argument, what she said, what you said, and what was the deep dog house result. Following this pattern, use "argument shorthand" and describe two recent arguments you had with your wife that left you in the deep doghouse.

Deep Doghouse Argument #1

Persons involved: _____

Reason for disagreement: _____

_____

What she said: _____
_____
_____

What was said by others, if anyone else was present: _____
_____
_____
_____
_____

What I said: _____
_____
_____
_____
_____
_____

Deep doghouse result: _____
_____
_____
_____
_____
_____

DEEP DOGHOUSE ARGUMENT #2

Persons involved: _____

Reason for disagreement: _____
_____

What she said: _____

What was said by others, if anyone else was present: _____

_____

_____

_____

What I said: _____

_____

_____

_____

_____

Deep doghouse result: _____

_____

_____

_____

_____

Hopefully, by now you are already beginning to recognize what you might have done differently in these two events that might have helped you avoid the deep doghouse. But just to be on the safe side, let's at least partially replay these events, employing the first rule of deep doghouse communication: *No matter what the issue is, the correct answer is, "You are right."* Especially for anger addicts, this is the best and probably the only way to avoid an anger escalation that will land you in the deep doghouse. And when in doubt, add CBSSW phrases just to make your position clear.

Going back to Louse and Richard, let's pick up just the last part of their scenario.

Instead of saying what he did, he could have said: *Honey, you are right. It is just wrong of me to put you in a risky situation with that car.*

Possible Non-deep doghouse result: *No fight, Richard gets to keep his truck and his wife, and somehow Louise is going to end up with a better car, too.*

Now, go back and rewrite your two arguments. Rewrite what you might have said so that it conforms to the rules of deep doghouse communication. Then predict what a possible outcome might have been if you had followed these rules at the time.

DEEP DOGHOUSE ARGUMENT #1—NEW ENDING

Instead of saying what I did, I could have said: _____

_____

_____

Possible Non-deep doghouse result: _____

_____

_____

DEEP DOGHOUSE ARGUMENT #2—NEW ENDING

Instead of saying what I did, I could have said: _____

_____

_____

Possible Non-deep doghouse result: _____

_____

_____

Well, as they say, it looks good on paper. And you probably even get the point we are trying to make. But old habits are hard to break. Old attitudes are hard to unlearn. Old arguments are hard to let go of. And on top of that, the blame honestly shouldn't *always* fall on you. Just because you are the guy with the anger problem doesn't mean you are the one who starts all the arguments. We know that, and you know that, but try telling that to the police or to the workers from child protective services. Try telling that to the judge at the divorce hearing. All these people know is that you are the guy who went ballistic at one o'clock in the morning and woke up the whole neighborhood and scared his wife and kids half to death. You may not be the guy who starts all the arguments. But *you are the guy who is going to pay the price* if you don't develop a different pattern of communicating during those arguments.

How about a little "psychological ping-pong?"

One of the ways to teach yourself not to get sucked into dangerous arguments with your wife, or with anyone else, for that matter, is to learn how to play "psychological ping-pong." To be really good at this game, all you have to do is find a way to *agree with some part* of a negative statement that someone (usually your wife) says about you. You don't have to agree with all of it. You don't even have to agree with the main point. But you have to try to find a way to agree with something about the statement, instead of turning it into an excuse for an anger event.

At the point when she makes a negative or critical remark about you, begin your replay with "You are right." Then briefly explain why she is right.

Here is an example to get you started. Suppose your wife asks you to vacuum the living room to help her get the house ready for dinner guests coming in the evening. You initially say no, because you have already ordered a pizza and are just about to sit down to watch the University of Oklahoma and the University of Texas play football on TV. Then she zings you back with this comment:

"You are just selfish and lazy. You never do anything around here to help me."

Of course, you see things differently. You remember fixing the garbage disposal when it jammed last week because she tried to put watermelon rinds through it. And you remember coming straight home from softball last Thursday instead of hanging out with the guys because she needed you to help sand that old rocking chair she got at a garage sale. You remember a lot of things, and right now you want to tell her every one of them. But instead, you will say, (in the quietest and calmest tone of voice you have):

"You are right, dear. I was being selfish for putting the game ahead of helping you. I will have the vacuuming done in plenty of time for the party tonight."

And that is how psychological ping-pong is played. It is important to work just as hard at this game as you would at any other competitive event, be it a sport or your job. Of course, the point of this exercise *seems* to be to lose, and that is hard on most men, especially anger addicts. We have been hurt plenty of time ourselves, and when someone takes a swipe at us, we feel like we must stand up for ourselves. But remember, your most important job is to *stand up to yourself first*. Don't let anger win. When you win at psychological ping-pong, it may *look* like you have lost an argument; it may even *feel* like you have lost an argument. But you have won a big victory against anger.

Now, for your first big test. In the spaces below, list as many of your wife's complaints or criticisms toward you as you can remember. These might have come up in recent arguments, or they might be standard problems for which she has been ragging on you for

Chapter 3 • *Put a Sock In It* 111

years. After listing each complaint, practice your new skill at psychological ping-pong to respond with an answer that will keep you out of the deep doghouse.

1. My wife says I _____
_____
_____

She is right because _____
_____
_____

2. My wife says I _____
_____
_____

She is right because _____
_____
_____

3. My wife says I _____
_____
_____

She is right because _____
_____
_____

4. My wife says I _____
_____
_____

She is right because _____
_____
_____

5. My wife says I _____
_____
_____

She is right because _____
_____
_____

    Now it is time for the baptism by fire. Some guys might find this next step a little intimidating, but if you have made it this far, you are ready for this test. In the space below there are places for your wife to write down three attitudes or behaviors she feels you need to change or improve. Just hand her the book, tell her that it would be very important to you if she could be as honest as possible. Explain to her that you are working very hard to make changes and this would be very helpful to you.

One behavior or attitude I wish my husband would improve or change is: _____
_____
_____
_____

A second behavior or attitude I wish my husband would improve or change is: _____
_____
_____
_____

A third behavior or attitude I wish my husband would improve or change is: _____
_____
_____
_____

    After your wife returns the workbook to you, read over each listing several times. Be aware of your anger levels. If you feel yourself getting too tense and angry, set the book aside for a little while. Come back to it later when you have calmed down. But don't put it off too long. Even if it is uncomfortable or upsetting, you have now been called up to the Big Leagues of psychological ping-pong. And the ball is in your court.

After you have studied each of your wife's comments, your job is to write a reply that will fit the rules of the game. Remember, the purpose of this exercise is not to humiliate you or blame you or make you feel like a failure. The goal is to help you learn to respond to your wife during tense situations in ways that will turn down your anger, and keep you out of the deep doghouse.

Here we go:

First comment

My wife is right because _____

_____

_____

_____

_____

Second comment

My wife is right because _____

_____

_____

_____

_____

Third comment

My wife is right because _____

_____

_____

_____

_____

From the Baptism of Fire to the Moment of Truth

The final step in this exercise is the hardest and the most important. Can you go back to your wife and share your responses with her, face to face? Of course you can. Will it be easy? Certainly not. But you do it, and do it well.

After you have finished your responses, practice reading them out loud to yourself. You need to hear yourself say these words and get used to the way it feels when you say them. Next, ask your wife to give you about 10 minutes so you could share something with her that you have been working on. Right before you meet with her, spend a few minutes alone to get focused. Try to take several slow deep breaths as we described in the section on meditation in Chapter Two. Then, when you sit down with her:

1. First explain to her that all she is supposed to do is listen. She doesn't need to respond to your remarks; just let you share them with her.

2. Then, tell her thank you for being patient with you and helping you with this assignment.

3. Now you are ready. Go back to the first comment and, beginning with, "You are right because ...," simply read the responses you have written down.

4. After you have finished all three responses, tell her thank you again. You are done. Do not try to have any further conversation at this point. You are still breathing. Maybe you are on your way to staying out of the doghouse.

Moving On To Shallow Doghouse Communication

After working your way through that last minefield, this next section should be much easier to handle. Shallow doghouse communication really has two distinct applications. First of all, it is very helpful for getting you the rest of the way out of the doghouse and back into a safer and more satisfying relationship with your wife. Second, this form of communication is also very useful in *keeping you out of the doghouse in the first place*! Learning to recognize how and when to use the key ideas and phrases we will be working with here can improve your entire marriage by 200%, maybe more.

Let's begin by working on dealing with past offenses. Stop for a moment and think about anything you have done recently – stretching back over the past 6-8 weeks – for which you have not offered a sincere, no-excuses apology. Rageaholics should have no problem thinking of at least three, so pick the top three. Events for which *you tried to apologize* in a way that was *so lame and insensitive* that your wife refused to accept it are also eligible for this list.

Briefly describe each event below:

Event one

When did it happen: _____

Where did it happen: _____

Who was involved: _____

What I did or said that still requires an apology: _____

_____

_____

_____

_____

Event two

When did it happen: _____

Where did it happen: _____

Who was involved: _____

What I did or said that still requires an apology: _____

_____

_____

_____

Event three

When did it happen: _____

Where did it happen: _____

Who was involved: _____

What I did or said that still requires an apology: _____

_____

_____

_____

Now, take just a minute to study our list of key shallow doghouse phrases one more time:

"I am really sorry."

"It was all my fault."

"Please forgive me."

"What can I do to make it up to you?"

Keeping these phrases in mind, let's work on writing apologies for each of these three events. Don't try to make this into something complicated. It is really simple. Just name the place and date where it happened, identify each of your behaviors that caused pain to those involved, and use any or several of the phrases above. Check out the example below:

Cynthia, I have been really thinking about Monday night. I am really sorry for the way I yelled at you and the kids at the game. It was all my fault. Could you please forgive me for embarrassing you and hurting your feelings?

Now, using the spaces below, compose sincere apologies for these three events. Remember, *do not use any form of the deadly phrase, "if you were upset …"*

EVENT ONE

Apology for event one: _____

_____

_____

_____

_____

_____

_____

_____

_____

Event two

Apology for event two: _____

_____

_____

_____

_____

_____

_____

_____

_____

_____

Event three

Apology for event three: _____

_____

_____

_____

_____

_____

_____

_____

_____

_____

Facing the music

You have come this far. You might as well go all the way. We can guarantee you that your wife would still like to hear a decent, well-thought out, sincere apology for each of these events, even if it has been months since the event took place. You now have these apologies ready to roll, hot off the press. Now is the time to ask your wife for another appointment. Expect this one to last longer than 10 minutes. Allow 30 minutes, because she may want to respond in some way to your apology. If she does, be sure to listen carefully and be ready to *mirror* what she says to you.

How to mirror your wife's comments

This is a great communication tool, once you learn how to use it. And it is so simple. Just listen very carefully to what your wife is saying to you. About every three or four sentences, ask her in a very kind voice if you can make sure you understand what she is saying to you. At that point, just repeat back to her what you heard her say, as close to word-for-word as you possibly can. Here's a quick example:

Bonnie: *I am so frustrated with you because you always want to sleep late on Sunday, and the kids and I really want you to go to church with us.*

Chuck: *Let me make sure that I understand what you are saying. I am hearing you say that you are upset with me because I want to sleep late on Sunday instead of going to church. Is that right?*

At that point she will either say yes or no. If she says no, ask her to repeat her last comments, and mirror them again. Keep doing this until she says, "Yes, that's it." Couples who make a habit of being this careful when communicating on delicate topics are much better at avoiding arguments that those who are so busy thinking about what they are going to say next that they don't pay a bit of attention to what is being said.

Back to your apologies

After mirroring her comments, you may discover that you have a few more things to apologize for than you realized. But don't worry. Just keep these phrases handy:

"I am really sorry."

"It was all my fault."

"Please forgive me."

"What can I do to make it up to you?"

If necessary, be ready to use deep doghouse phrases, too. You might try "You are right, I was wrong," or any of the CBSSW phrases. Don't defend or excuse anything. Stick to your main message: *"I am really sorry. Would you please forgive me?"*

Be sure that you ask, "What can I do to make it up to you?" for each offense before moving on to the next one. And remember to accept whatever she asks for without complaining or resisting.

It's the thought that counts

We can't promise that your wife will accept your apologies, kiss and make up. We can't guarantee that this will immediately get you out of the doghouse or keep you out of the doghouse. But that is not really the purpose of this exercise. What you are really trying to accomplish here is to do something constructive with your words instead of causing more pain. All you can do is practice humility and offer a sincere apology. It may take awhile for things to begin to smooth out.

There is always the possibility that too much damage has been done over too many years for a marriage to be restored, even after hard work like this. *But doing the work is still important.* By working on your anger here and now, you will greatly improve your chances for happiness and satisfaction in the future.

Remember, there is a God and you are not Him

Before we end this chapter, this might be a good time to remind yourself that you are just a guy trying your best to change, and that you need all the help you can get. Learning how to think and communicate in these new ways feels strange, maybe even wrong. There are going to be hard days and you are going to make some mistakes along the way. We don't expect you to be perfect, and neither does God. The important thing is to keep trying. Don't give up.

If you would like to, use the space below to write a letter to God. Ask Him for the strength to do the things that are hard and scary. Tell Him you are once again giving up your need to be in control of anything. Admit that you are powerless to change without His help. Ask Him to help you remember that you are not in charge of trying to change your wife, either. And don't forget to ask for His help for any specific need or concern that you may have.

Dear God,

_____

Signed   Date

CHART Your Progress

You should still be charting your progress at abstaining from banned behaviors, as well as working with your note cards from Chapter Two. We don't want to load you down with too much more paperwork, but there is one important area that would really be good for you to track.

The following chart contains a list of key phrases for effective shallow doghouse communication. Make enough copies of this weekly chart to last for the rest of your 90-day training period. Make a concentrated effort to use these phrases as often as you can, whenever it is appropriate. At the end of each day, put a check mark beside every one that you were able to use that day. At the end of each week, tally up the number of times you used each phrase.

Do you find any that are "underworked?" Which ones do you use most often? Are you satisfied with the results you are getting? Is there anything you could do to use these phrases – along with similar ones – more effectively?

Week of _____ to _____

"SHALLOW DOGHOUSE" COMMUNICATION CHART"

MAKE ADDITIONAL COPIES

Chart Your Progress in Shallow Doghouse Communication

Phrase								
"You are right."								
"I really am sorry."								
"It was all my fault."								
"Please forgive me."								
"What can I do to make it up to you?"								
"I see you are still upset with me. I would really like to hear about it."								
"When you are ready to talk, I promise just to listen."								
"Let me see if I understood what you said. Did I get what you said?"								
"Thank you for sharing with me. I really appreciate it."								
"In the future it would please me if you would…"								
"Honey, thank you so much for …"								
"I love you; you are the most beautiful woman in the world."								

Slips, Wins and Miracles

For an anger addict, getting anger under control sometimes feels like trying to nail Jell-o™ to the wall. It's just not easy to do. Every minute is full of challenges and you never know where the next one is coming from. For example, review the round-by-round description below of the way one addict started a typical day. Pay attention to the way he talked himself through some ticklish situations.

ROUND #1 (This was easy... just answer the question.)

God gave me a pop test coming out of a sleep; not a good time for people with anger problems.

The other morning my cell phone, which I keep by my bed, rang at 7:00 AM about an hour before I usually get up. I work until 9:00 in the evening.

I answered and this guy asks, "Is this the plumbing supply place?"

His words are slurred as if he had been coming off an all night drunk.

I say, "No, it's not the plumbing supply place," and the guy hangs up.

ROUND #2 (Not a problem... I can handle this.)

In 20 seconds the phone rings again and it's the same guy asking, "Is this the plumbing supply place?"

Again I explain that he has the wrong number and again he hangs up. I congratulate myself on a job well done. I even think that it is funny of all the numbers in my area code, he calls the anger therapist twice.

I do stay near the phone. Why? Because I'm dealing with a guy who dials the same number twice, and gets the wrong party, and hangs up without saying "excuse me" and doesn't bother to check the number in the book or call directory assistance. I just have this nagging suspicion that I could hear from him again.

ROUND #3 (This one runs my anger meter up.)

The phone rings again. I am begging to slip. By then I am irritated enough to answer the ring with, "This is still not the plumbing supply place, pal." [Sarcasm and name-calling: -10 points]

Is he embarrassed or offended? Why no. He just says, "I'm tryin' to get Doug's Plumbing Supply." [Inside my anger gauge is at 9 on a scale of 10]

I ask him what number he's dialing. He tells me, and –*surprise!* -- it's *my* number. So, I explain to him that he's dialing the number of my cell phone, not Doug's Plumbing Supply. But you are not going to believe the next part.

He challenges me. He suggests that I don't know my own phone number! He says, "That's the number Doug gave me to call *his* place." I tell him he must have misunderstood the number.

[All my training is starting to kick in. I am deliberately talking very softly, determined not to blow up or to get condescending, AND my anger feelings are going down!]

ROUND #4 (I have got to let <u>him</u> be right.)

"I got it written down, right here," he argues.

At this point I have to decide whether to hang up and quit answering the phone, or try to help the guy. Maybe the latter course will be better for me, as well as for my friend on the line. So, I tell him he needs to look up the plumbing supply place in the phone book and get the right number.

ROUND #5 (At this point I know God is behind this and I resolve to hang on to the end to measure my progress.)

"I'm in this booth," he says. "Ain't no phone book in here." I tell him to call directory assistance then.

ROUND #6 (I hate this even worse... asking not-so-smart questions. I feel personally humiliated.)

"Call what?"

I explain about directory assistance, how it used to be called Information, how you talk to an operator and say you need to call Doug's Plumbing Supply and they give you the number.

ROUND #7 (At this point, my wife wants to check my driver's license to make sure an alien did not invade my body. What did they do with her hot-headed husband?)

"I ain't got no more change," he says. Hmmm. Must be because he's already called my number three times.

At last I find myself doing what I wish I had done when the guy first called. Here I am, before breakfast, locating my glasses and getting out the Yellow Pages to look up a phone number for Doug's Plumbing Supply.

ROUND #8 (Now he wants to argue with the Yellow Pages!)

I ask the guy if he has anything to write with, like a pen. He says yes – thank you, God for small miracles -- and I tell him to listen carefully, and write down the following numbers. I read them off slowly, but I am simply not prepared for the next remark that comes out of his mouth:

"That ain't the number *Doug* told me to call."

(Stay calm, stay calm.) I tell him I *know* it's not the number he's been calling. That's the whole problem. Probably, he just wrote Doug's number down wrong. It's very similar to my cell number; only off by one digit.

ROUND #9 (Another stupid question... by now I am thinking in profanity, but sounding like a saint still.)

"One what?" he asks.

One digit. One number. That last number is a seven and not a nine. Did he get the number written down?

"Oh sure, I got it right here."

All right, I now tell him to hang up and go find a convenience store, or some other place where he can get some change, or where somebody will let him use a phone, and call Doug at the number I just got through giving him. I tell him to throw away that other number he's been calling because he'll never get the plumbing supply place that way. Did he understand? He says sure, and fades away.

I even end up feeling pretty good about going to all that trouble to help out an old boy who's obviously operating under a handicap. But I should have expected this:

ROUND #10 (End of test. Sorry, God. I am not up to 10 more rounds... maybe next time.)

About an hour later my phone rings again and I hear, "Is this the plumbing supply place?"

I don't respond, but hang up and turn off my phone. That is the best I can do for today!

An anger addict always has more work to do! I would give myself a "B" on this one. Four calls are three more than I would have handled without an explosion ten years ago.

A Process, Not an Event

We like to remind people that recovery is a process, not an event, meaning that you work on your anger control issues every minute of every day, week after week, month after month, year after year (a *process*). Once you choose to accept the fact that you have an anger problem, that doesn't magically solve the problem right then and there (that would be a one-time *event*.) You have to **keep choosing to not lose control** over and over again, sometimes – as you can see from the story we just read – numerous times in the same conversation! And because we are human and because this is a process that never stops, we have good days and bad days. No one is expecting you to be perfect. You need to expect to keep working on this the rest of your life. Over the long haul, **you will get better.** But every day will be a battle. Below is a little checklist to help you keep track of your progress.

Use this scorecard to record your response to the anger control challenges you will face every day. Make as many copies as you need. Write the new date in the blank each day. Under *slips*, make a note every time you fail to abstain from one of the 15 banned behaviors. Under *wins*, note times when you still expressed angry feelings, but didn't slip back into a banned behavior. Under *miracles*, note any time that you felt angry but were able to do the opposite of how you were feeling on the inside. Good Luck!

Slips, Wins and Miracles

My Daily Anger Control Scorecard For _____

Slips

Summarize Situation and list banned behaviors) you used: _____

_____
_____
_____
_____
_____
_____
_____

Wins

Summarize Situation and list banned behaviors you wanted to us but didn't: _____

_____
_____
_____
_____
_____
_____
_____

Miracles

Summarize situation and describe how you did the opposite of what you felt: _____

_____
_____
_____
_____
_____
_____
_____

Part II

A New Strategy for the Women Coping with Angry Men

"I'm not angry that your mum butts into our marriage, but I'm angry that she's right with her babbling!"

CHAPTER 4

Facing Facts: *Un*happily Ever After?

Megan stared blankly at the police report. The counselor at the station was kind and patient. She gently reminded Megan that this was simply the first step in trying to get her and the kids the help they needed. But Megan was having a hard time concentrating. To some degree it was because her neck was still sore and stiff, and her shoulder really hurt. But mostly, she was just numb, in shock. She just couldn't get her brain around the facts of the past six hours.

Donny just lost it today. She thought he was doing so much better. He was showing more interest in the kids, he was helping more around the house. His last real rage event, the one where she and the kids ran across the street to the neighbors, had been almost four months ago. In fact, it had been almost a year since the last time the police came out. (They had come to the house three times in the past two years.) Going to AA had really helped him cut back on his drinking. He hardly ever brought home a six-pack anymore. Oh, she had overlooked a few things that could have gotten ugly, but they turned out to be minor. She had been trying really hard to do things that she thought would please him. And she thought it was working.

But this morning, just as she and the kids were getting ready to leave for school, day-care and work, they had another "incident." She had to go out to his truck to get a bag of kitty litter he brought home from the store, and while she was rummaging around she found something that looked suspiciously like marijuana in a baggie under the seat. She took it back in the house, showed it to him, and asked him where it came from. He immediately got tense and told her it belonged to his brother Tommy, who must have left it there last Saturday when he borrowed the truck.

I should have just said "Okay" and dropped it right then and there, Megan thought to herself now, in retrospect. *But I had to go and open my big mouth.*

Actually, what she had said was, "Donny, please get rid of this stuff and don't let Tommy use your truck anymore. You know that if the police find this stuff anywhere near you, they are going to violate you. The conditions of your probation from the last time they came out order you to abstain from the use of any alcohol or drugs."

And that was all it took. Donny exploded at her, ordered her to leave his brother out of this and quit telling him how to run his life. Megan turned to leave the room; she and the kids were going to be late. But Donny lunged for her, grabbed her by the left arm and jerked her back toward him. When she resisted, he threw her to the ground, got on top of her, grabbed her neck with both hands, and began to choke her. He was yelling obscenities and telling her he was sick and tired of her self-righteous attitudes.

Their oldest child, Christina, age 9, came running in. When she saw what was going on, she ran to the phone and called 911. The operator had just come on the line when Donny slapped the little girl and knocked her to the floor. Megan jumped up to defend Christina, and when Donny resumed choking her, Christina grabbed Charlie, age 5, and shot out the front door and across the street to the neighbors. Fortunately, the neighbors had already heard the commotion and called 911 themselves. The police were there in less than two minutes. They pulled Donny off of Megan, put him in cuffs, and hauled him off to jail.

Now Megan was sitting in a dumpy little waiting room, trying to fill out a police report that would certainly send her husband to jail, at least for awhile. She was really tired and really sad. **Most of all, she felt like a huge failure.** She had tried so hard. And still it had come to this. At that moment, she flashed back to that point in the fight where Donny had slapped Chrissy to the floor, and Megan clearly saw the terror in Chrissy's eyes. She would never forgive herself if anything ever happened to the kids. Suddenly she knew what she had to do. Slowly, more like a robot than a person, she starting filling out the report. And as she worked her way through the paperwork, she paused just briefly to ask the social worker how she could get in touch with a good divorce lawyer.

Is this a true story? Probably, even though it is not based on any actual single case file. It is true because this kind of tragedy happens somewhere close to you, maybe right in your town, maybe right on your street, countless times every day. Maybe it has happened – is happening – right in your own home. If that is the case, then please pay very close attention to what we are about to share with you.

The Biggest National Epidemic You Never Heard Of

In the winter of 2003, the entire world was in an uproar over the outbreak of a new disease called SARS. It originated in China and gradually spread around the world, throwing public health officials into a state of absolute panic. SARS viciously attacks the respiratory system and is often fatal, especially in older patients or people with weakened immune systems. All during the spring of 2003, the world rallied together to halt the spread of this dreadful disease. It was on the national news every night. Twenty-four hour news channels interviewed expert after expert in their attempt to inform the public and help them protect themselves. The epidemic seemed to ease toward the end of May. In July, the Associated Press reported that the epidemic had been contained. The worldwide death count from this sinister killer – 812 persons, mostly in China and its neighbors, with a handful scattered across Canada and Africa. Very scary stuff.

Now, compare that number with this one. In one year (1998) 4,189 women were killed by their intimate partners, with 58% of the deaths being married women killed by their husbands. ***Four thousand, one hundred and eighty nine women*** killed in **one** country in **one** year. Compare that to 812 deaths *worldwide* from SARS – a disease that was fairly easy to contain in a matter of months – and decide for yourself what we should consider to be the bigger threat, the real epidemic. Yet, aside from brief coverage on the Police Blotter page of the newspaper, or a 30-second blurb on the late night news, violence against women goes largely unrecognized for what it truly is – one of the most lethal health problems a woman in America can face. Unfortunately, comprehensive statistics do not exist that would document the number of women who are simply terrorized, battered, bruised, maimed or injured as a result of family violence. But we can tell you this much: at the center of each tragic incident is an angry man.

Just the facts, m'am

Just read over the following family violence summary, and try to comprehend something that is truly incomprehensible.

FAMILY VIOLENCE FACTS AND FIGURES

- ✓ Between 21 and 34 percent of American women are battered by a male partner.

- ✓ Between 24 and 30 percent of battered women lose their jobs because they can't be at work due to emotional trauma or physical injury.

- ✓ 56 percent of abused women are harassed by the abuser at work.

- ✓ For statistics current through 1998, more than three out of every 100 women (1.8 million) had been severely assaulted by male partners during the past year – punched, kicked, choked, beaten, threatened with a gun or knife, or injured by a gun or knife.

- ✓ Other estimates put this number at between 8.5 and 11.3 percent of the American female population.

- ✓ At least 16 percent of American couples experience assault every year.

- ✓ Nearly one in eight husbands carries out one or more acts of violence toward his partner every year.

- ✓ One-third of all female family violence victims receive serious physical injuries.
- ✓ 20 to 30 percent of women seen in emergency rooms showed signs of physical abuse. Half of these admitted the injuries were inflicted by their partners.
- ✓ 10 percent of the victims were pregnant at the time of the abuse.
- ✓ 86 percent of the victims had been abused at least once before.
- ✓ 40 percent of those previously injured had required medical attention for those earlier abuse episodes.
- ✓ Practically all victims of physical abuse report troubling instances of emotional or psychological abuse. In one survey of 234 abuse victims, 98 percent reported emotional abuse and 72 percent agreed that the affects were even more damaging than the physical abuse.

What is WRONG with this picture?

One of the most widely debated topics in the study of family violence is the question of why so many women stay in such bad relationships. It is clear that it cannot be dismissed as a function of education or socioeconomic status. Rates of abuse for women who are college educated, with house-hold incomes of $100,000+ are just the same as for women without a high school diploma living in households making less than $30,000 a year. Some may be too afraid to leave. Others may not have the kind of outside support system to help them leave. Many women stay for the sake of the children, or because they still love the good parts of their husbands, even though they hate the bad parts. Many women become numb to the violence and the anger, even though they hate it. They learn to tiptoe around it and survive it so staying ends up seeming like the best of a lot of bad options. Then there are some, like Megan in our story, who have tried so hard for so long to make it work that they just won't allow themselves to wake up, give up, and walk out. Their fear of failure is too high.

ASSESS Your Current Relationship

Perhaps the one thing all of these women have in common is being confused about when to stay and when to leave. Is it possible for an abused woman to tell when it is too dangerous to stay another minute? How do you know when to keep working on your marriage and when to start working on a divorce? If you are wrestling with these questions right now regarding the angry man in your life, and especially if someone else gave you this book because they are concerned about what you are going through (even though you are still hanging in there), then a good place to start is by filling out this questionnaire.

REALITY CHECK FOR WOMEN LIVING WITH ANGRY MEN

Answer each question by circling either "yes" or "no." If you are not sure, or if it doesn't apply to you, just leave it blank.

Yes   No

☐   ☐   Do you have arguments in which your partner becomes loud, angry, aggressive, and threatening?

☐   ☐   Does your husband often blame or criticize you?

☐   ☐   Does he complain often about the way you look, dress, cook, keep house, or raise the kids?

☐   ☐   Does he make cruel jokes about you or use sarcastic, cutting remarks when talking to you or about you?

☐   ☐   Does he criticize you in front of friends?

☐   ☐   Does he generally have a short fuse, one moment seeming fairly normal and then, with very little provocation, over-reacting with an extreme, hostile outburst?

☐   ☐   Do you and the kids walk on eggshells at home, trying not to upset him?

☐   ☐   Do you sometimes blame yourself for triggering his angry outbursts, saying things like, "If only I had …. (kept dinner warm, kept the kids quieter, spent less money at the grocery store, etc.) he probably wouldn't have been so upset"?

☐   ☐   Does he usually have the last word in an argument?

☐   ☐   Has an argument ever turned into a physical fight between you and your partner?

☐   ☐   Has there ever been a physical fight during a pregnancy?

☐   ☐   Are you often afraid of your partner?

☐   ☐   Have you ever made up a cover story to explain evidence of physical abuse (bruises, scratches, scrapes, black eyes, sprained muscles, etc.)?

☐   ☐   Have you ever made up a story to cover up the emotional affects of abuse (things like depression or anxiety)?

☐   ☐   Do you ever excuse his angry, violent behavior on the basis of the fact that he is under a lot of stress at work, or that he had a very bad childhood, or that he experienced trauma during military combat or some other tragedy?

☐   ☐   Has your partner ever threatened to hurt you?

☐   ☐   Has your partner ever threatened to hurt your children?

☐	☐	Have you ever left your partner, or tried to leave, because of domestic violence?
☐	☐	Does your partner prevent you from leaving home, using the telephone, seeking contact with family/friends, or otherwise control your activities?
☐	☐	Does your partner destroy your possessions or hurt things you value, including household pets?
☐	☐	Does your partner use drugs or alcohol when he abuses you?
☐	☐	Has your partner ever threatened to harm himself?
☐	☐	Has your partner ever assaulted you (punched, kicked, hit, pushed, choked)?
☐	☐	Does your partner ever force you to have sex?
☐	☐	Has your partner ever threatened to use a weapon against you (gun, knife, hammer, or other object)?
☐	☐	Has your partner ever used a weapon against you?
☐	☐	Have you or others ever called the police because of something your husband did or was doing to you?
☐	☐	Have you ever gone to a doctor or hospital due to injuries caused by your partner?
☐	☐	Do you ever use drugs or alcohol as a way to cope with your husband's anger or abuse?
☐	☐	Have you ever asked for help to stop the abuse, such as from police, a court order, counseling, support groups, shelter, family, friends, clergy or other outside help?

Rating Your Risk

Now, go back and count how many questions you answered with "Yes." Write that number here: _____.

Before we proceed to the next step, if you have a close, trusted friend or family member that is generally aware of your situation, ask that person to go over this questionnaire with you and see if they would agree with the way you answered these questions. If they think you didn't say Yes to enough questions, go ahead and write in the number of extra questions they think you should have answered with a Yes right here _____. Add this number to the number you wrote down.

For example, if you answered Yes to ten questions but they found six more that they think should have been Yes, the total score you should use is **16**.

Adding both scores together, your new total is _____.

Use the figures below to assess the seriousness of your situation:

If your score was between **0 and 2**, your relationship is probably normal, perhaps just a few loud disagreements from time to time.

If your score is between **3 and 5**, your relationship is probably physically safe, but anger is an issue in your relationship that could use some attention. However, if any of your Yes answers were for questions involving threats of violence or actual violence, it would still be a good idea to check with a family violence counselor or other helping professional to get a second opinion.

If your score is between **5 and 10**, there are definite risk factors here for serious abusive episodes and possibly even violence. You are in trouble, whether or not you are willing to admit it. Maybe you are blaming yourself or making excuses for him, but this is not good and it could get worse with very little warning.

If your score is between **15 and 20**, you are already very aware that you are in trouble, but you just don't know what to do about it. Maybe you still love him or you think staying is best for the kids. Read this out loud:

*My staying in this situation is **not** good for the kids. Loving him doesn't mean staying with him and allowing him to hurt us. It is time to do something.*

We recommend calling a close friend or a helping professional and arranging to start working on your situation immediately

If your score is above **20**, hopefully you have already separated from your partner, moved to a shelter, called the police and had him arrested, and/or filed for divorce. Nothing else is going to keep you safe or help you save your marriage.

THE TRUTH HURTS

There it is in black in white. Can your marriage be saved? Do you want it to be saved? We don't have answers to those questions. But we do know that it is probably not going to get better, and that is bad enough. It could get worse. And the only one who can do anything about it right now is **you**. The chances of your husband changing on his own are slim to none. At this point, it may seem to him that he is getting away with whatever he wants to. Why should he change?

Maybe at some point someone told you that you can't change another person, you can only change yourself. That is not completely true. It is very possible that if *you* make some very hard but important changes, your husband might get motivated to change in a way that he hasn't been up until now. It is possible to "inspire" him to want to change. But first we need to dig a little deeper.

PIT BULLS AND COBRAS

Many years of research into the nature of abusive relationships has taught us that these relationships are driven by a complex set of emotional, psychological and sociological factors. In addition, different people have different anger profiles and different trigger mechanisms. However, for the purposes of this workbook, we can say that, in spite of the factors that make each relationship unique, abusers generally fall into one of two categories. It is very important to understand which group your man fits into before we develop a plan for your situation. The abuser's basic anger behavior pattern provides the key to sorting this out.

The first group is called ***Pit Bulls***, and just like the dog breed of the same name, they can be really nasty and very dangerous. However, just like most dogs, they can be trained. If you are married to a Pit Bull and you think you still love him, training might be an option. But be aware from the beginning that the process will require a lot of courage and strength on your part, and it doesn't always have a happy ending.

Pit Bull abusers become angry, and sometimes violent, because they are incredibly, desperately insecure. They are emotionally dependent on their wives and have an intense fear of being abandoned. Their solution is to control and dominate their wives in every way they can think of in an attempt to keep from losing them. During arguments or anger events, Pit Bulls exhibit physiological responses consistent with the "fight or flight" syndrome we mentioned earlier in this workbook. Their heart rate, respiration and blood pressure all increase. They feel threatened, so their bodies prepare for battle. Eventually, they erupt in some sort of explosive anger event. They will do anything to try and control the women they feel they can't live without. Often the things they do are foolish, reckless and dangerous. Besides bitter, hysterical and irrational outbursts of emotionally abusive anger; besides punching walls and breaking furnishings; and in addition to grabbing, slapping, choking and punching; Pit Bulls can become stalkers.

However, it is the desperate fear of losing the woman he needs that makes a Pit Bull trainable. He is accustomed to using anger, fear and even physical domination to intimidate her into submission. And he will continue to do those things over and over and over again as long as she lets him get away with it. However, if she is willing to stand up to him, using a variety of options at her disposal, his overwhelming desire to keep her in his life *might* be a motivator for change. The options are not easy or simple. They include:

- Calling the police and filing charges against him whenever he is violent.
- Demanding that he leave the house and filing for a protective order to keep him out.
- Strictly observing the rules laid out in the protective order.
- Turning him in to the police when he violates the protective order.
- Demanding that he receive counseling or enroll in an anger management program, assuming a judge hasn't already done so.
- Refusing to let him return home until he has demonstrated, over a significant length of time, that he is committed to change and has already made significant changes.
- Filing for divorce.

It may be necessary to take the children and leave the home before attempting any of these other options. Services for victims of family violence, including temporary shelter and regular counseling, are available in most areas. It is a good idea for a woman in an abusive relationship to be in some sort of counseling or support group, even if her husband refuses. She will need wise, consistent support to hold up under the stress of this "training" program. It is very easy to fall for his old charms and new sob stories, and end up letting him come home too soon. You already know what that is like. You have probably already been through it at least once.

This strategy is not guaranteed to work in all situations. But it is guaranteed to work better than whatever it is you have been trying up to now. You are the one who must decide what you want to do next.

MY HUSBAND GETS ANGRY A LOT, BUT HE HARDLY EVER GETS VIOLENT.

There is a class of Pit Bulls who have a definite problem with anger, but they always seem to stop just short of physically violent behaviors. They definitely have a short fuse; their anger can quickly rage out of control and become irrational. They do a lot of screaming, accusing, and name calling. They are prone to door slamming, wall punching and tire squealing. They often make what we call "$500 reactions to $5 problems." They blow situations all out of proportion and create a crisis where none really exists. Their anger may be causing more problems for them at work than at home, because they have a tendency to feel like certain people are just against them all the time. If you scored between 5 and 10 on your Reality Check test, you may be married to a Pit Bull who fits into this class.

However, the fact that this particular class of Pit Bull rarely, if ever, becomes physically violent actually makes the situation harder to deal with. You probably tell yourself that his anger problem isn't all that bad because he has never hit you or the kids, and you can always patch the hole in the bedroom wall. In the meantime, you and your children walk on eggshells around him all the time, especially if he is under stress at work. You make excuses for him to the kids, the neighbors and your family. When he is having an episode, you try to pretend nothing is wrong, calm him down and wait for things to blow over. Living with this kind of stress and anxiety takes a very high emotional and psychological toll on a family, especially on children as they grow and mature. But since the anger leaves no physical marks, it is easier for you to minimize, while the emotional scars grow ever deeper.

Remember, a few pages back we mentioned that 98% of women who had been physically abused reported that they had also suffered emotional abuse, and 72% of those said the emotional abuse was even more damaging that the physical violence. Let's think about that for a minute. How does emotional abuse produce such severe damage?

Every rage event has a trigger; every anger addict needs a target to justify his attacks. The target is often an innocent bystander like his wife or one of his children. Whoever it is, this person is more than simply a target. She is actually going to become the *Scapegoat*, and she will be blamed by the addict for causing his anger. Make no mistake about it, she is not the cause, **she is the victim**!

It works like this: The rageaholic comes home from work 45 minutes late and his supper is cold. His wife had it ready on time, because the last time supper was late he went into a rage. But tonight he was 45 minutes late, so she had to go ahead and feed the kids *and get the 3-year old in the bathtub. She intended to get back to the kitchen and warm up his meal before he came in, but they were out of clean towels and she had to stop and find some and get the baby in the tub. By the time she got back to the kitchen, it was too late. He is home and hungry, and the meal definitely does not meet with his approval. He launches into an angry tirade, accusing her of every sort of wifely malfeasance and dumps the food on the floor. He then orders **her** to clean up the mess and make him something fresh and hot and now! The wife is in tears, the kids are all cowering in the bathroom and the husband is recharging in the kitchen. No one knows what is going to happen next.*

Notice, he never got around to throwing any punches or breaking any dishes. But, this is horrible for several reasons. First of all it creates a delusion on the part of the rest of the family that his anger is **their** fault. **They** must find ways to do better and think faster in order to keep him happy. Practically the first thought that a rageaholic's wife will have after an anger event is, "If only …": If only she had kept the supper warm, if only she had supper ready on time, if only she had kept the kids quiet because he had a headache, if only she hadn't spent so much at the market … *The if onlys never stop*! They are all lies anyway, because serving a cold meal to someone who is 45 minutes late and who didn't even call to let you know is not grounds for severe anger abuse. The Scapegoat is the Victim in this story, and in this marriage. **But there are other victims, too.**

Cowering in the bathroom are three little kids, ages 7, 5, and 3. They are all scared, but they are already learning to pretend that they don't hear anything, because they have heard it too many times before. But for the 3-year-old, it is especially scary. Not only did he hear Daddy get really mad at Mommy, but he also heard Mommy say the supper was bad because *she was busy putting the baby in the tub*. To a 3-year-old, this is concrete evidence that the whole thing is *his* fault. **He** is the reason Daddy is mad; **he** is the reason Mommy is in trouble. And that can only mean that **he is bad**, because **he** caused this whole mess.

Children who grow up listening to the rantings of a rageaholic father are all consumed with this fear of being blamed or punished. They just assume that any time something goes wrong, they will pay the price. Their stomachs begin to twist into knots whenever they hear Dad's car pull up in the driveway. They run for their bedrooms the minute they hear his voice begin to get loud. They try to make themselves invisible so they won't be the Scapegoat for any of his attacks, but it is inevitable that they will be targeted sooner or later.

Remember, a rageaholic is looking for excuses to rage. There is nothing you can do, nothing you can fix, nothing you can improve or change or rearrange that will control his anger. He will make an excuse to blow when he is ready to blow, and the target is likely to be whoever is closest at the time. Because of this, children from abusive families grow up infected with what John Bradshaw calls *Toxic Shame*. It is a chronic sense of being permanently flawed, of being bad, feeling there is no hope of ever being truly normal. It eats at these people all of their lives. Most of the time they feel anxious, stressed, afraid, ashamed and, as they get older … very angry. As adults, many of them become rageaholics, or marry rageaholics.

So, even if your rageaholic doesn't actually hit you or choke you or send you to the hospital, his anger is still extremely destructive to you and your kids. You may never have to call the police on him, and you may be uncomfortable filing for divorce, but it is important that you hold him accountable for his behavior. **He can be trained**. Ask him to take anger management classes; ask him to seek counseling; be willing to leave the house for several days to dramatize the seriousness of the situation. But don't sit there and do nothing! Your marriage will be stronger, your life will be happier, and your children will thank you if you take action **now.**

WHAT CAN YOU DO TO TRAIN A COBRA?

Stop for just a minute and try to remember when was the last time you went to the circus to see the trained cobras. That's right. There is no such thing! You can't train cobras. They are cold-blooded killing machines that use cunning, stealth, hypnotic techniques and lethal poison to conquer their prey. The best thing to do when you see a cobra on the loose is to get as far away as you can, as fast as you can. If you are married to a Cobra, the same advice still holds.

Abusers who are classified as Cobras are entirely different animals from the Pit Bull. The most startling difference may be physiological. Unlike the Pit Bull, when a Cobra gets ready to strike, he doesn't get loud and aggressive and agitated, working himself up slowly but surely to a violent outburst. His heart rate, blood pressure and respiration actually goes *down* instead of up. He becomes calm and focused before striking out in ways that are even more ferocious and frightening because they seem coldly calculated. A Cobra isn't motivated by desperation or fear; he is motivated by a pathological desire to control and destroy. It is not unusual for Cobras to have a history of criminal and/or anti-social behavior. And in spite of all their genuinely scary qualities, they often have an amazing hold over the women in their lives.

We don't have any suggestions for healing relationships where Cobras are involved. If you believe you are hooked up with a Cobra, our only advice is for you to get out as fast as you can, and seek the assistance of a therapist who can help you work on getting your own life back together.

SO, WHAT'S IN YOUR BEDROOM?

Perhaps you already have a pretty good idea of which category your husband falls into, but just to make it official, take a minute to answer the following questions by putting a check in front of each question that comes closest to fitting your situation.

___1. I can usually tell when my husband is building toward a rage event.

___2. My husband sometimes does things that seem downright cruel, just for fun.

___3. When my husband is angry, he really gets out of control, going on and on in almost irrational ways, maybe even breaking things.

___4. When my husband calms down after an anger event, he is often very ashamed and apologetic, and does something nice for me to make up for it.

___5. When my husband gets really quiet and tense, it makes me very anxious.

___6. My husband has always been kind of a loner. He doesn't have many close friends and doesn't seem to want any.

___ 7.   When my husband gets angry, his face turns red, his breathing gets faster and he breaks out into a sweat.

___ 8.   My husband sometimes hurts me, either physically or with very cruel remarks, without ever raising his voice or giving me any warning that he was upset.

___ 9.   My husband rarely shows even the tiniest hint of regret after he has hurt me in some way. What apologies he offers, if he ever does, are short and feel very insincere.

___ 10. My husband is constantly wanting to know where I have been, whom I have talked to, when I am going to be home and what I am going to be doing. He strongly resents anyone or anything that interferes with our time together.

Questions 1, 3, 4, 7 and 10 fit the profile of the Pit Bull. How many of these questions did you check? Put that number here _____.

Questions 2, 5, 6, 8 and 9 more closely apply to Cobras. How many of these questions did you check? Put that number here _____.

The results of this test are not intended to be scientific proof that your husband fits into either category. Some men will certainly have characteristics of both groups. But if you circled as many as four questions in either group, this is a big hint about what you may be dealing with. What happens next is up to you.

BREAKTHROUGH TO A SAFER, SANER LIFE

Very often, women who are in relationships with angry men have lost all perspective on what a happy marriage could be like. They definitely don't like dealing with the anger events, but they have learned to survive them. They have taught themselves to just look on the bright side and find something positive to focus on. Or they devise elaborate survival mechanisms that involve trying to prevent arguments before they start, or maybe even deceiving or working around their husbands somehow, all in an attempt to control his anger. Women like this are true survivors, but they are not truly happy. They gave up on that a long time ago.

Would you like your marriage to be happier? Just for the record, let's look at what you would like to see happening in your marriage and family, and compare that to what is actually happening. The questionnaire below contains a list of 16 items that many women say increase their satisfaction and happiness in marriage. After each item, circle the number that comes closest to matching how important this item is to you.

1 = Not very important
2 = Sometimes important
3 = Kind of important
4 = Very important
5 = Extremely important

MY IDEAL MARRIAGE

1 2 3 4 5   I want my husband to be interested in me and how my day went instead of only being interested in what he wants and how he feels.

1 2 3 4 5   I want my husband to consult me about important family decisions rather than just telling me stuff at the last minute.

1 2 3 4 5   I want my husband to listen to my feelings and concerns without getting upset or trying to fix me.

1 2 3 4 5   I want my husband to hold me and comfort me when in I am sad or hurt, without being mad at me or lecturing me.

1 2 3 4 5   I want my husband to listen to my ideas, and take them seriously, instead of ignoring them or making fun of them.

1 2 3 4 5   I want to be able to tell my husband what I really need and how I really feel without being afraid that he will react with anger, sarcasm, or complaints.

1 2 3 4 5   I want my husband to be excited for me when something good happens for me at work or another activity I enjoy.

1 2 3 4 5   I want my husband to help around the house without making me feel like I am a failure for not getting it all done on my own.

1 2 3 4 5   I want my husband to touch me and hug me affectionately, without making me feel as if every touch is supposed to lead to sex.

1 2 3 4 5   I want my husband to be tender and loving when we have sex instead of making me feel as if I have to be a porn star.

1 2 3 4 5   I want my husband to be understanding when I make mistakes instead of criticizing me and making me feel stupid.

1 2 3 4 5   When we have differences of opinion, I want my husband to listen to my point of view without interrupting or criticizing me.

1 2 3 4 5   When we have disagreements, I want my husband to be willing to be open to the possibility that I might be right some of the time, and be willing to compromise.

1 2 3 4 5   When we have a discussion, I want my husband to control his tone of voice and body language, and treat me with respect.

1 2 3 4 5   When we have disagreements, I want my husband to be careful not to say or do things that will scare or upset the kids.

1 2 3 4 5   When we have disagreements, I want my husband to refrain from trying to "win" by getting aggressive or physical with me in any way.

Now, go back and look at your answers to these 16 questions. How many questions did you answer by circling 3, 4, or 5? Count them and write that number in this blank _____. These questions represent the things that you value most in marriage. Having these things happen regularly in your marriage would probably help you to feel better about yourself, your marriage and your life.

Now we are going to compare what you would like to happen with what is really happening. The following questionnaire will help you measure how often these important things are actually taking place in your marriage. We will use the same numbering system, except this time the numbers will represent how often your husband does each of these things in your marriage.

0 = Never
1 = Rarely
2 = Infrequently
3 = Sometimes
4 = Most of the time
5 = Always

My Marriage By The Numbers

1 2 3 4 5   My husband is interested in me and how my day went instead of only being interested in what he wants and how he feels.

1 2 3 4 5   My husband does consult me about important family decisions rather than just telling me stuff at the last minute.

1 2 3 4 5   My husband accepts my feelings and concerns without getting upset or trying to fix me.

1 2 3 4 5   My husband does hold me and comfort me when in I am sad or hurt, without being mad at me or lecturing me.

1 2 3 4 5   My husband listens to my ideas, and takes them seriously, instead of ignoring them or making fun of them.

1 2 3 4 5   I can tell my husband what I really need and how I really feel without being afraid that he will react with anger, sarcasm, or complaints.

1 2 3 4 5   My husband is excited for me when something good happens for me at work or another activity I enjoy.

1 2 3 4 5   My husband helps around the house without making me feel as if I am a failure for not getting it all done on my own.

1 2 3 4 5   My husband does touch me and hug me affectionately, without making me as if every touch is supposed to lead to sex.

1 2 3 4 5   My husband is tender and loving when we have sex and doesn't

make me feel like I have to be a porn star.

1 2 3 4 5   My husband is understanding when I make mistakes and doesn't criticize me and make me feel stupid.

1 2 3 4 5   When we have discussions, my husband listens to my point of view without interrupting or criticizing me.

1 2 3 4 5   When we have disagreements, my husband is willing to be open to the possibility that I might be right some of the time, and is willing to compromise.

1 2 3 4 5   When we have differences of opinion, my husband does control his tone of voice and body language, and treats me with respect.

1 2 3 4 5   When we have disagreements, my husband is careful not say or do things that will scare or upset the kids.

1 2 3 4 5   When we have disagreements, my husband does refrain from trying to "win" by getting aggressive or physical with me in any way.

To score this exercise, go back and count all the questions where you circled either 4 or 5. How many did you find? Write the answer here _____.

Now we want to compare these results with the score on the previous exercise — *My Ideal Marriage* — where you counted how many answers you circled with a 3, 4 or 5. On the spaces below, write in both the scores from that exercise and the one you just completed.

My Ideal Marriage score _____

My Marriage By The Numbers score _____

Take a long hard look at both of these numbers. How big is the difference between them? Are they fairly close together — maybe a 12 for the first score and a 10 for the second? If so, then the chances are good that your marriage is pretty strong and making changes in the future will be challenging but successful.

But what if there is a big difference between the two numbers – maybe you had a 12 for the first score but a 2 or 3 on the second score? Sadly, this is usually the way it goes when you are in a relationship with an anger addict. But over the years, women in these relationships end up counting very small blessings instead of working for real improvements. You know what it is like:

You tell yourself that things are starting to get better because he hasn't really yelled at you or the kids in over a week.

You are really happy because he agreed to let you go visit your sister for the weekend.

He told you that supper tonight "wasn't too bad."

He only told you that he hated your new haircut, he didn't actually laugh at you.

Stop counting small blessings. Start paying attention to the Big Picture. There is a very big difference between a 3 and a 12 when it comes to being happy and healthy in your marriage and your life. These numbers don't lie. And they can change. Your husband can change. Your marriage can change. But the chances are very good that nothing will change **unless you are willing to change, too.**

EXAMINING THE EVIDENCE

Think back to the most recent big blowup that happened between you and your husband. Do you remember what happened? Do you remember how it made you feel? Let's replay it one more time, and see if we can learn anything helpful from it. First let's study this example:

Nita and Jason had just gotten home from a Saturday afternoon shopping trip to the mall. Jason was bringing packages in from the car and Nita went into the kitchen to start supper. She quickly discovered that she was out of cooking oil, and she needed it to fry the chicken strips she had planned for the meal. When Jason finished bringing in the packages, she asked him sweetly if he would mind going to the market to pick up the oil. He immediately stiffened and Nita could sense what was coming next.

"We just got in from driving around town all afternoon!" Jason snapped. "Why didn't you stop and pick some up then? Why wasn't it on your list? And, since you are the one who screwed up and forgot to get it, why should I be the one to get back out in the car and push my way through the moron parade at the store?"

"Jason, I'm so sorry," Nita said quietly. "I would be happy to go back and get it, but that would only delay supper longer and I know you are hungry. I could be working on the salad and potatoes while you are gone and ..."

"Well, that's just great!" bellowed Jason. "We are all starving. Now supper is going to be late. The whole thing is your fault, and you are trying to pin it on me? Nita, you are such a screw-up! I don't know why I even put up with you. You and the kids can stay here and play house if you want to, but I am out of here. At least at Wendy's they have all the ingredients to make a decent meal!"

And with that, Jason stormed out of the house, got in his truck, and peeled out of the driveway. He came home sometime after midnight.

In the meantime, Nita stood in the kitchen for a while and just cried. She couldn't understand why Jason always said such mean, unfair things to her. How could he say he loved her and yet treat her like this? This was not all her fault! But he made everything her fault. And she just didn't know what to do.

Now, let's break this down into a few basic parts. Here is what we need to know:

Anger Event

Who was involved: Jason and Nita

When did it happen: Saturday afternoon

Where did it take place: At home, in the kitchen

What was the trigger (the issue that started the argument): Nita needed oil for supper and asked Jason to pick some up at the store.

What happened next: Jason got angry, criticized Nita and called her names, then stormed out of the house, leaving her and the kids alone for the rest of the evening.

This left Nita feeling: rejected, blamed, humiliated, confused, hopeless

Now, pick a recent anger episode involving you and your husband. If it also included other people, that's fine, too. Describe the event, using the space below:

ANGER EVENT

Who was involved? _____

When did it happen? _____

Where did it happen? _____

What was the trigger? _____

_____

What happened next? _____

_____

_____

_____

_____

_____

This left you feeling: _____

_____

Let's be perfectly clear about one thing here: *It is normal to have disagreements, even heated arguments, in marriages that are happy and healthy.* It is not the disagreement that is the problem, it is how the disagreement is handled that can cause problems. The goal of this workbook is not to cause you and your partner to always agree. Instead, we want to help you both learn to **disagree** in ways that are safe and productive, so that the disagreement can be solved without turning into a disaster.

So let's take another look at the anger event you just described, and talk about what we wish might have happened. Let's use Jason and Nita's story to give us an example. We already know all the details; let's just add one final category that we will call:

It would have been so much better if:

Jason could have expressed his feelings without raging. Nita would have felt better and the whole evening would have been saved if Jason had said something more like, "Nita, I am really tired, and I am not very happy to find out that we don't have everything we need for this meal. Is there anything we can substitute for the chicken strips? No? Well, I will go and get the oil, but in the future, please plan ahead a little better."

Nita felt a little sad that her negligence had inconvenienced Jason, but she was glad he was willing to help out. She went to work on supper and looked forward to a quiet night at home.

Notice that this is not a storybook ending. We could have inserted a cheerful happy, Jason kindly consoling his wife, telling her not to worry because everyone makes mistakes then have him stroll out the door whistling a merry tune all the way to the store. We aren't saying that something like that couldn't happen. But in the real world when people are grumpy and tired, there is nothing wrong with settling for simply solving the problem without yelling so you can get on with your life.

Now, go back and rewrite the ending of the anger event you wrote about above.

It would have been so much better if: _____

_____

_____

_____

_____

_____

If it had turned out this way, it would have made me feel: _____

_____

_____

Get the picture?

Let's do one more short exercise. Words can't really tell the whole story when a family is in crisis. You can learn a lot from facial expressions and body language. In the space below draw a picture of what your family looks like during the first hour after a big rage event. Assume this space is your family room. Show where each member of the family is most likely to be sitting, what they might be doing, and indicate the expression on each face. This does not have to be great art. Use stick figures and label whatever you think you can't draw. We just want to see what you see.

Now, the final step: draw one more sketch. This time, use the space to draw what you wish your family looked like, at home together on any given night.

Don't give up on the hope that this second picture can come true for you and your family.

Chapter 4 • Facing Facts

THE POWER TO CHOOSE

You have worked very hard in this chapter, but there has been a purpose. We wanted you to take a long, hard look at what you really have in this relationship. We wanted you to take a step out of your old mindset and start to think about is really happening. We wanted you to think a little bit about what it could be like if things started to get better because now you have to look at some hard choices.

We have already told your husband in the section of this book that *the more he does what he always did, the more he will get what he always got.* The same is true for you. Are you happy with what you have been getting? If not, the only way to get something better is to do something different. But it won't be easy, and nothing we offer here is guaranteed to magically heal a relationship. Sometimes things are too far gone. Sometime people just quit on you half way through the journey. But more often than you might expect, **people will change.** People can change if they have to.

THE TEETER-TOTTER EFFECT

Remember when you were a kid riding the teeter-totter with someone else? What happened when you suddenly got off the teeter-totter? Bam! They hit the ground hard! What if you simply shifted positions – moved farther up or farther back? The other person had to move, too, in order to keep things in balance. Or they could just quit playing. That choice was always open. It still is.

Right now, you have an opportunity to change the balance on the teeter-totter that is your marriage. If you change your position in some key areas, your husband will have to change, or quit the game. You will never know what you could get until you do something different.

HARD CHOICES

Below is a set of brief anger scenarios. Each scenario has a suggested response for you. Simply write "yes" in the blank after each option you would be willing to choose.

- *In the middle of an argument, your husband shoves you over the coffee table and on to the floor, injuring your shoulder and breaking the glass table top. You receive scrapes from the glass. Before leaving the room, he threatens to bash your brains in if you mess with him any more. Would you be willing to call 911 and report an assault and a terroristic threat?*

  _____

- *The police come. Your husband says it was all a big misunderstanding and wants to apologize. Would you be willing to file charges anyway?*

  _____

- *Your husband erupts in a fit of hysterical anger because of the high amount of the electric bill. He accuses you and the kids of wasting electricity and wasting money. This is the third time this week he has jumped on you and the kids. Would you be willing to tell him he must seek counseling immediately for his anger problem or you will take the kids and leave?* _____

- *At the next anger eruption, would you be willing to take the kids and leave?* _____

- *After you take the kids and leave, your husband agrees to go to counseling. Would you be willing to ask him to find another place to live while he is getting counseling?* _____

- *He has been in counseling for three months. You and the kids see him about three nights a week, but he is still sleeping somewhere else. He says he is ready to come home and begs you to let him stay. If you weren't completely satisfied that he was in control of his anger, would you be willing to say "No, not yet"?* _____

If you can say yes to most of the options listed above, you are ready to learn how to become a trainer. Only time will tell if your husband will be a good student.

MY PROMISE TO MYSELF

As a way of closing this chapter, write a letter to yourself in the space below. Promise yourself that you are ready and willing to choose a different, safer and wiser path in dealing with your partner's anger and the consequences it has had for you and your family. Tell yourself anything else you need to say in order to get you ready for the next step in this journey to a safer, saner life.

Dear _____

_____

_____

_____

_____

_____

_____

_____

_____

_____

Signed   Date

"I agree it was a pointless arguement, but I still won."

Chapter 5
The Line In the Sand

She and Dan had been married for 15 years. They had four kids and a nice house and good jobs and a pretty good life. But Dan's horrible rage attacks, which had been a problem from the very beginning, had just gone from bad to worse. While they were dating it had only been really bad once. During the first five years of their marriage his Category 5 outbursts (a few years back, Liza started grading his attacks like tornados or hurricanes, on a scale of Category 1 through Category 5) gradually increased in frequency, going from one about every three months to about once a month. From then on he seemed to average two or three per month. But in the past six weeks she and the kids suffered through eight eruptions, all over stuff that was petty and ridiculous. She asked him to consider going with her to counseling. That triggered attack number four in the series, which pushed her into doing something she knew she should have done a long time ago: she went to counseling by herself even though when she did it triggered attack number five.

She and her counselor had agreed that Dan's anger was taking a terrible toll on her and the kids, and that the chances of his deciding to change voluntarily were extremely remote. He helped her develop a strategy for presenting Dan with an ultimatum, including very strict boundaries that she was prepared to enforce until he showed signs of making serious improvements. She had agonized long and hard over this; she had prayed and cried and looked for alternatives. There didn't seem to be any. She desperately wanted everyone in her family, including Dan, to find peace and joy for their lives. There was no guarantee that this plan would fix everything, of course. Still, she was so tired of the abuse; she was devastated by the look of pain and fear in her children's eyes after each rage event. She was ready to take the risk.

She was glad about one thing. Her counselor suggested that she ask Dan to attend just this one session. They agreed she would explain to Dan that in order for the counselor to have a clear understanding of how to help Liza with her "problems" her therapist needed to ask Dan a few questions. Dan was very glad for the opportunity to go and help get Liza straightened out. So here they were, sitting in the relative calm and safety of the therapist's office. Dan was on his best behavior. At least for the moment.

Therapist: Dan, thanks for coming in this afternoon. I know you had to rearrange your duties at work.

Dan: Well, I am glad to help if I can. Just as long as this doesn't drag on too long.

Therapist: I don't think it will. Actually, all you need to do right now is just sit back and listen. I want to start by asking Liza to read something she has written. Liza, you're up.

Liza: (swallowing hard) Dan, before I say anything else, I want you to know that I love you very much. The things I am about to share with you are only intended to help our marriage and our family become stronger, happier and healthier. (She was surprised at how calm she sounded; calmer than she felt, that's for sure.) Now, I have come to some decisions I want to share with you.

I have decided that the way you express anger around me and the kids is hurtful, irresponsible and destructive

Because it is hurtful, irresponsible and destructive, I have decided I will no longer tolerate your inappropriate expression of anger around me and the kids at any time for any reason.

Dan: (interrupting) Hey, what is this! I thought ...

Therapist: (interrupting Dan's interruption) Dan, I will make sure you get a chance to respond in a minute. But Liza has to finish her assignment first. Liza, go ahead.

Liza: (another deep breath) I have decided to ask you to begin anger management therapy immediately, giving serious attention to correcting the behaviors on this list. (She handed Dan a list of 12 behaviors she wanted Dan to change.)

Therapist: (noticing that Dan's face was starting to turn red) Take a deep breath Dan, we are almost done with Liza's part. Then it will be your turn. This is very important. Go ahead, Liza.

*Liza: Finally, I have decided that if you don't begin counseling **immediately**, I will immediately take the kids and go stay with my folks. I will apply for a protective order that will require you to move out of the house and prohibit you from contacting us. If you still make no effort to deal with your anger, I will file for divorce. I don't want to, but I will. I have already talked to a lawyer. Please take this seriously, because I am serious.*

With that closing warning, she was through. With a calm demeanor that belied the collage of surging emotions she felt in her stomach, she quickly got up and left the room. By the time Dan could recover enough from the shock to shout at her, "Liza, what the hell do you think you are doing?" She was gone. She had arranged for Julie to be waiting to pick her up and drive her home. She had already started packing. What she did now would be determined in the next few minutes. Her therapist would call her and give her a report. In the meantime, she would just sit by the phone and wait.

*Therapist: Okay, Dan. **Now** is your chance to respond. What are you going to do next? Why don't we at least take a look at this list?*

CAN I REALLY CHANGE HIM?

*How many psychotherapists does it take to change a light bulb? Only one, but the light bulb has **to really want to change.***

This old joke points out a basic principle of most counseling models that says you can't tell people what to do, you can only help them find out what they really want to do and then help them get there. Because of this, a lot of women believe — erroneously — that there is nothing they can do to get their husbands to change. This is simply not true. Sure, you can't wave a magic wand and cause him to instantly become a completely different human being. But it is very possible to *motivate him to want to change*, or at least to be willing to change. That's what this chapter is all about.

Most Pit Bulls are terrified of separation. They are emotionally dependent on their wives. The real, serious, unrelenting threat of separation will very often provide the motivation that he needs to finally face his problem and work to change it. But if you want to go there, you have to know how to play the game.

THE RULES OF THE GAME

Rageaholics are great at playing games. They excel at manipulation and intimidation. They can make you laugh; they can make you cry; they can scare you to death; and they are ready to use physical force if necessary in order to get what they want. Their goal is to control the women in their lives, and they play to win. Sometimes those women decide two can play that game, but whenever they try, they hardly ever win. Their attempts to threaten and intimidate usually fail for one simple reason: they aren't willing to play the game to win.

It is not unusual for women who are married to anger addicts to threaten to leave, or threaten divorce. Sometimes they will call the police, and often they will apply for protective orders. Sometimes they will take the kids and move into a shelter. As a result, many of the men in these relationships begin to soften and repent; they make promises and some might even go to counseling. All the while, these guys are also begging their partners: *Please get back together. Please come home (or please let me come home). We can't work this out as long as we are apart. How will you ever know I have changed unless we move in together again? We need each other. The kids need us together. Give me another chance. Please, I love you, I need you, I can't live without you.*

Eventually, this can start to sound really good to a woman alone. Money is tight, she has three kids in tow. She finds herself thinking things like: *He sounds sincere. Maybe he has learned his lesson this time. I'll give it one more try.* Inevitably, the minute he unpacks his bags, the cycle starts all over again. It may take a while for his rage to build back to full strength, but there is no doubt that it will. Because **he won again!** He got to come home on **his** terms. All he had to do was look sad, make a few promises, maybe go to a few classes and time his move just right. The game is control; his goal is to get her back in his life without giving up anything important. And she was no match for him.

How do you beat this guy? Change the game, change the rules, and **play to win**.

How To Get A Pit Bull's Attention

For the Pit Bull, the game is all about keeping his lady in his life. When women try to get in the game, too, *they make the mistake of playing for the same thing*. Because she may still love him, or for the sake of the kids, or for the sake of financial security, or whatever, she also wants to keep *him* in *her* life. She just wants him to be nicer, that's all. With that strategy, she will lose the game every time. She may take action to get him out of the house temporarily, and he may accept a few inconvenient consequences. But, after a little emotional shell game, he will eventually end up back in the house, **which is where he wanted to be all along!**

If you want to win, first you must change the game. The game can't be about getting him to be nicer, the game has to be about getting him to be **safer**. The whole point of your game must be to make life safer for you and your children! He can be nice whenever he wants to be. (That's how you ended up married to him in the first place!) *But that is not the same as being safe.* He has abused you emotionally and maybe physically. He has threatened you. He has damaged property and terrorized the kids. As long as you are looking for ways to help him be nicer so that you can stay with him, **you will lose**, and it won't be pretty.

The name of your game has to be **safety first**. He can be charming, he can even be truly sorry – and don't doubt for one minute that he won't try to convince you that he is all of that -- but that is not the same thing as being truly safe. If you are working on a plan for making him behave, the goal of the plan has to be making him a safe person to be with. The game is not over until you are convinced, beyond a reasonable doubt, that he has done every bit of the hard work necessary to assure you and everyone who loves you that he will never threaten the peace and safety of your home again.

If you are going to win, you have to change the rules. Up to now, the rules have gone pretty much like this:

*He gets angry, you get upset; maybe you even call the police because it gets ugly. But when the police come, he blames you or maybe he apologizes to you, but for whatever reason the police give you both a good talking to and they leave. Or maybe you don't even call the police, you just calm the kids down and clean up the broken dishes and try to pretend that nothing ever happened. Maybe you even went to a shelter once. But it was crowded and some of the people there had **real** problems, not like your situation, which usually calms down eventually. So you let him stew for a while, and when he said he would never do it again, you came home.*

So, in summary, the rules are:

Old Rules
- ✓ He has a rage event.
- ✓ You react with pain and sadness.
- ✓ You try to do something about it.
- ✓ You either pick a response that doesn't work, or you give in too soon.
- ✓ He wins, and the game begins again.

You have tried that stuff. It is a recipe for disappointment and disaster. There is a better way. If you want to win, here are the rules you will need to play by:

New Rules
- ✓ Don't wait until the next rage event. **Act now.**
- ✓ Give him orders that are crystal clear, outlining what he must do if he wants to keep this relationship.
- ✓ Enforce them immediately. No negotiating.
- ✓ Be prepared for lots of whining, complaining, raging, promising, apologizing, charm, and outrageous grandstanding, because it will come. Don't pay attention to any of it.
- ✓ Don't give in on any point until it is certain that he has his anger under control for good.

The rest of this chapter is devoted to developing and enforcing these new rules.

Play to win

This is the one game that the rageaholic does not know how to win. He is no match for a woman who knows what she wants, knows what she is doing, and *who won't stop until she gets it*. In short, he doesn't know how to win a game that he can't control.

Interrupt His Life For An Important Announcement

The key to success in training a Pit Bull is getting his attention. You have to announce your intentions and decisions in a way that he can't ignore or talk down. In this section you will plan your announcement strategy – everything you want him to change and what the consequences will be until he does change. You will need to be thorough, clear and firm. He may not be happy with your announcement, but he should have no doubt about what you are saying. Remember, he will be looking for any loophole or sign of weakness to manipulate to his advantage. You have to cover all the bases.

First Base: How Safe Are You Right Now?

The first thing that needs to be determined is the degree of risk you and your family are facing right now.

Yes	No	
☐	☐	Is your partner regularly and unpredictably violent?
☐	☐	Has he harmed or threatened to harm you in the past ten days?
☐	☐	Is he likely to harm or threaten to harm you in the immediate future?

If the answer to any of these questions is yes, then part of your plan, and part of your announcement, might call for asking him to leave the home immediately. You should also contact the authorities and ask for a protective order prohibiting him from having any contact with you, the children or anyone else in your immediate family. The announcement you are about to make to him is going to make him very scared and angry. If he is prone to violence, your plan must have a provision for getting him out of the house while he begins to work on his anger. Remember, Safety First.

If your partner has no history of threatening or committing physical violence, it is possible that you can implement your plan in a way that allows him to stay in the house, so long as he is keeping the rules. But the plan should also include a provision for requiring him to leave if he breaks certain rules.

Second Base: Behaviors He Must Change to Stay in a Relationship With You

This is the most important part of the announcement. You have to be absolutely clear regarding the behaviors you will no longer tolerate. He must be willing to stop them immediately if he wants to continue in a relationship with you. Below is a chart, taken from Chapter One of this workbook, which lists 16 behaviors that anger addicts have trouble controlling. If you need more information about these behaviors, feel free to turn back to Chapter One and study them more thoroughly. The chart has a place for you to check each behavior that you want him to stop. It also has a place for you to circle how often he does this behavior:

> A = Always
> O = Often
> S = Sometimes
> R = Rarely

You will also be asked to circle the number which best describes the intensity of the damage (emotional, physical, or psychological) he causes when he does each behavior:

> 5 = Extremely destructive
> 4 = Very destructive
> 3 = Definitely a problem
> 2 = Mild problem
> 1 = Irritating

Now, take a minute to fill in the chart below. This will help you determine the instructions you are going to give to your husband later.

PROBLEM BEHAVIOR	FREQUENCY	INTENSITY
☐ Speaking when angry	A O S R	5 4 3 2 1
☐ Staying when angry	A O S R	5 4 3 2 1
☐ Staring when angry	A O S R	5 4 3 2 1
☐ Interrupting for any reason when angry	A O S R	5 4 3 2 1
☐ Cursing any time, for any reason	A O S R	5 4 3 2 1
☐ Name calling, any time for any reason	A O S R	5 4 3 2 1
☐ Threatening	A O S R	5 4 3 2 1
☐ Pointing	A O S R	5 4 3 2 1
☐ Yelling, raising his voice, talking in a mean tone	A O S R	5 4 3 2 1
☐ Mocking and/or being sarcastic	A O S R	5 4 3 2 1
☐ Throwing things, slamming doors, banging walls	A O S R	5 4 3 2 1
☐ Non-affectionate touching	A O S R	5 4 3 2 1
☐ Telling "hero stories"	A O S R	5 4 3 2 1
☐ Sighing, clucking or rolling eyes	A O S R	5 4 3 2 1
☐ Criticizing and/or lecturing	A O S R	5 4 3 2 1
☐ Speeding	A O S R	5 4 3 2 1

Now, let's make another chart, one personalized for your situation. In the blanks below, list each of the behaviors that you checked above, but also include why you want it to stop. Explain how it makes you feel or describe the damage that it does. This is important because you want him to understand the pain he has caused. For example:

Behavior to stop: Speaking when angry.

Why it must stop: Because you get loud, you say horrible things that hurt me and the children, you get yourself all worked up and say things that don't make any sense and get totally out of control.

Now, it is your turn.

Behavior to stop:_____

Why it must stop: _____

_____

Behavior to stop:_____

Why it must stop: _____

_____

Behavior to stop: _____

Why it must stop: _____

_____

Behavior to stop: _____

Why it must stop: _____

_____

Behavior to stop: _____

Why it must stop: _____

_____

Behavior to stop: _____

Why it must stop: _____

_____

Behavior to stop: _____

Why it must stop: _____

_____

Behavior to stop: _____

Why it must stop: _____

_____

Behavior to stop: _____

Why it must stop: _____

Behavior to stop: _____

Why it must stop: _____

_____

Behavior to stop: _____

Why it must stop: _____

_____

THIRD BASE: WHAT HE MUST DO NEXT

Now that you have a list of the ways you want him to get his anger under control, you must provide specific instructions about what you want him to do next. This could include anything from reading this book, to enrolling in an anger management class (preferably one that is based on the principles discussed in this book), or going to therapy (using a model based on this book). And if, in order for you to feel safe, you need him to move out temporarily until his anger problems have stabilized, this is the place to mention that, too.

A word about psychotherapy: Many rageaholics could benefit from working on issues relating to childhood or to traumatic events that have occurred in their lives. However, this type of therapy can last for months or years, and it is **not required** in order for them to control their anger **now**. Don't allow your husband to hide from his responsibility to stop raging by getting lost or wasting time in therapy. Any anger addict who follows the principles outlined in this workbook can stop raging immediately. He can then spend the rest of his life working on other issues if he wants to.

In the space below, write out the things you want him to do next. The request should be clear, short and to the point. For example:

What I want you to do next is: Call this phone number, 555-1111, and make an appointment with David Wilson. Take this book with you and tell him you are there to get your anger under control.

What I want you to do next is: _____

_____

_____

_____

Home Base – Consequences For His Behavior

Now we are at home plate. This is where we score. This is where the game is won or lost. Up to now, you may not have done anything all that different from some of the things you have tried before. You may have asked him to work on his anger before. You may have given ultimatums before, or threatened separation. But somehow he got the upper hand anyhow and you folded. This time things will be different.

In this step, we will make a list of consequences that *you will enforce* if he doesn't cooperate with your requests. First, let's divide our options into two possible scenarios.

Scenario One – He is still living at home

If he is currently living at home, and you have not decided to ask him to leave as a condition of continuing to work on the relationship, then there is a broad range of consequences at your disposal:

- If he refuses to immediately and seriously agree to do what you requested of him in the previous step – make an appointment to get anger counseling, for instance – the consequence might be for him to leave the home, or for you to take the family and leave, and stay gone until he has made the appointment and attended at least two sessions. If he still refuses, your next step might be to file for divorce and get an order from a judge getting you back in the house and maybe ordering him into anger counseling.

- If he agrees to your requests, and you allow him to stay in the home, there may still be problems. He probably will have some relapses of banned behaviors. If they are serious and destructive – especially if they are violent, you must be prepared to *call 911, press charges and let him spend the night in jail*. Be prepared not to let him return home for as long as it takes until you are certain that you and your family will be safe around him.

- Even an anger addict who is making steady progress will occasionally slip up. Even though the slip-ups might not be violent or destructive, they still should not be ignored. If one of the banned behaviors on his list is sarcastic, hurtful wise-cracks, a failure to keep that rule might not demand that he move out, but there should be some price to pay. Washing dishes, doing housework, or anything that is unpleasant or inconvenient for him would be things to consider putting on that list.

Whatever the situation may be, *you must enforce* the consequences that you choose. If he doesn't believe that you are dead serious about these consequences, he will not stay serious about working on his anger.

Scenario Two – He is not living at home

If he is not living at home, then your situation is already quite serious. You are already separated. You may be considering divorce. You may already have some sort of court order in place to limit his access to you. The options under this scenario are very strict, and very important:

- ❏ If he refuses to comply with your request to take anger management, be prepared to file for divorce and request a protective order.
- ❏ If there is a protective order in place, **do not** give him permission to make contact with you, even if he is acting "nice" or looking sad.
- ❏ If he violates the protective order, document the violation and report it to the police immediately. If he comes onto the property where you are, don't negotiate or reason with him, call 911.
- ❏ Take every threat seriously. Call 911 immediately.
- ❏ If he threatens suicide, don't reason with him. Call 911 immediately.
- ❏ Emphasize to him that there can be no relationship until he has demonstrated to you, his counselor and any officers of the court who may be involved that his anger is clearly under control.
- ❏ If he continues to violate your requests and/or the orders of the court, going through with the divorce may be your only choice. He always has the option of working on his anger, and if he does, there may be other options later.

YOUR TURN AT BAT

Before we leave this section, make a list of the consequences you will use if or when he fails to comply with any of the requests that you have made. Just fill in the blanks below:

If he refuses to take anger management classes, or otherwise refuses to take seriously the requests I have made for him to work on his anger, I will: _____

_____

_____

_____

If he has a major, destructive rage event while living at home I will: _____

_____

_____

_____

Consequences that I might require if he violates any of the banned behaviors in ways that are not major or destructive include: _____

_____

_____

_____

_____

If he gets threatening or violent with me, I will: _____

_____

_____

_____

_____

If he is violent and the police respond to my 911 call, I will: _____

I will then let him spend: _____

If he violates a protective order, I will: _____

_____

_____

_____

_____

If he threatens suicide, I will _____

_____

Announcing Your Decision

All of the work you have been doing for the past several pages is to prepare you for presenting your demands to him. Now you have to plan how, when and where that will take place. Let's start with how.

How to organize your announcement

This process breaks down into steps that conform to the work that you just did. Everything you want to tell him should be prepared in writing, even if you intend to communicate some of it verbally. Having everything written down will prevent you from getting distracted or forgetting something important. And you will both have something written down in black and white to refer to later. At the end of this chapter we have included a worksheet that you can use to organize your entire preparation. Just fill in the blanks, use it to refer to during your announcement, and hand him a copy at the end, just so there can be no misunderstandings.

A. Begin with a clear, direct statement of your decision, along the lines of the one that Liza used with Dan in our opening story. Remember that one?

I have decided that the way you express anger around me and the kids is hurtful, irresponsible and destructive. Because it is hurtful, irresponsible and destructive, I have decided I will no longer tolerate your inappropriate expression of anger around me and the kids at any time for any reason.

B. Then present him with your list of behaviors you want him to immediately change or stop, including the reason why each one is hurtful to you or the family.

C. Now you are ready to tell him what you want him to do next.

D. Finally, tell him what the major consequences will be if he does not immediately take steps to comply with your requests. You don't have to lay out all of the consequences you wrote about in the previous exercise. Just include the most immediate and important ones.

When to make your announcement

The short answer here is, *just as soon as you can get ready*. He is not going to get any better at controlling his anger if you wait. You can't really predict what he will do next or when he will do it. Consult with your counselor, your pastor, your family and friends, or anyone else that you trust to help you get prepared. But as soon as the preparation is complete, do it is as fast as you can. Don't look for a convenient opportunity. There will never be one.

In the blank below, write down the time you plan to make your announcement:

I will make my announcement on or before _____

Where to make your announcement

There is a short answer here, too: wherever you feel most *safe*. You are the best judge of this. If your husband rages, but has no history of violence, you may be able to make your announcement to him at home, preferably at a time when the kids aren't around. Depending on how volatile you expect his reaction to be, you might invite a trusted friend to be present during the announcement. But if there is any possibility of violence, it would probably be better not to do it at home, and you should not attempt this alone. Meet at your counselor's office, or at your pastor's office, or even your lawyer's office.

Perhaps you do not have access to a good support system, or you have no one to stand with you when you make your announcement. As a last resort, prepare a detailed letter containing all the things that we have worked on here. Arrange to have this letter delivered to him in way that guarantees that he will receive it and read it. (In other words, don't just leave it on the kitchen table and expect him to find it and read it. He might do both, burn the letter and swear he never saw it.) Then contact him by phone and discuss the contents with him.

This is the location or the method I will use to make my announcement to him: _____

_____

_____

_____

_____

THE NEXT STEP IS YOURS

If you have worked your way this far through the chapter, you are obviously motivated, which is very good. You are also probably more than a little worried about what is going to happen next, which is very normal. We can't promise you what the outcome of your announcement will be, but we can assure you that you are now very well prepared to take that step. Congratulations on being willing to do whatever it takes to give your family a chance to be safe and your marriage a chance to survive.

Contracting for Cooperation

Depending on the safety level of your relationship, and the willingness of your partner to participate in the process, a simple contract can sometimes be a big help in controlling anger. If he is living at home and appears to be willing to work on the issues you have requested, the contract would help to build an extra level of safety and control around any potential anger events. The contract should have two parts.

> *Part One:* You and your partner agree that if you are engaged in a disagreement and he is getting angry, one of you should take a time out. That means one of you will leave the room and won't come back for as long as an hour. If the conversation can't be resumed without anger, call another time out or drop the subject. No cursing, door slamming, name-calling or sarcasm allowed either.

> *Part Two:* You and your partner agree that any time you interrupt your husband, he **must** quit talking and let you speak. This is one way to quickly turn off his anger motor, which is easily revved up as he goes on and on about something that is bothering him.

Sample Contract for Cooperation

I hereby declare and promise that:

A. Any time my wife detects that I am beginning to get angry, I will agree to an immediate time out. We will cease speaking and one of us will leave the room. I agree to abstain from all banned behaviors. We will not resume the conversation until she agrees that the anger has subsided.

B. I will allow my wife to interrupt me while I am speaking any time she detects that my speech pattern or subject matter is likely to lead to an anger event. I will not protest the interruption or attempt to regain control of the conversation. If necessary, I will take a time out.

_____   _____

Husband's signature   Date

_____   _____

Wife's signature   Date

The Battle Begins

Anger addicts are – above all – addicts. They depend on anger to give them a sense of being in control of the world around them. They even get a physical high from the anger experiences. They do not know how to function without anger, and they do not want to learn how to function without anger. They have developed a set of habits, emotions, and thought patterns that rely on anger as their primary coping mechanism. For all of these reasons, the rageaholic will have a battle on his hands when he finally makes a serious commitment to change. Even on the days when he intends to do his best, he may still slip and fall. This will not be an easy battle for him to win, which means that this will also be a difficult battle for you.

FIGHTING THE GOOD FIGHT

Even after your husband agrees to every demand you have made of him, and even after he has begun attending anger therapy, you must be prepared for the fact that he will have setbacks. They may not all be of the violent variety, but every time he fails to fulfill the requirements you have set out for him, it increases the likelihood that he will fail again that much sooner. That is why you must plan now for how you will respond then.

The following exercise will help you to think through how you will handle a couple of likely battlegrounds. Begin by thinking of two problem issues that usually produce some sort of wrong anger response by your husband. Pick one moderate example and one severe example. The idea of this exercise is for you to visualize each event from start to finish – time of day, location, people involved, nature of the issue, what he says and does, what you say and do, and how you might feel afterward.

Let's start with the moderate scenario first. Study the example below:

Nickie had just picked Max up from work. His car was supposed to be ready by close of business today, but the parts didn't arrive in time, so he was without wheels, which always made him stressed. And he was ticked at the repair shop guys because they had promised him they would have the car out today. They should have told him there might be problems getting the parts! As he slid in behind the wheel of Nickie's car and she slid over to the passenger side, he was also stressed about something else: he had to ride home in rush hour traffic with Nickie. She was such a right seat driver, always telling him to watch out, slow down, don't get so close, blah, blah, blah. Being with her today would make a miserable commute even more miserable.

Nickie was not unaware of what was going on in Max's head. She could sense his frustration, and she was well aware of his tendency to drive angry. That is why she had designated angry driving as one of the behaviors he had to agree to stop doing when she presented her demands two weeks ago. She knew today was going to be a big test.

Max knew that she knew how he was feeling, and he had not forgotten the agreement they had. He took a deep breath, and pulled out onto the access road and headed for the freeway. Traffic was already bumper-to-bumper. He squeezed his way into merging traffic, wisely avoiding the temptation to honk his horn. They hadn't driven more than a mile when traffic came to a dead stop. He could see flashing lights up ahead and knew they could be trapped here for an hour. Realizing this was his last chance to avoid being stranded in freeway Hell, he gunned the engine and whipped out of his lane, careening down the shoulder and shooting through a tiny hole next to an 18-wheeler. His intention was to make the next exit, get back on the access road, hit the light at 51st, and cut over to River Road. But at the very last second, the driver of the 18-wheeler had the same idea. Not seeing Max in his side-view mirror, he swerved toward the exit. Max jammed on his brakes, squealed his tires, shouted a string of obscenities and hit his horn, all in one motion. And at that instant, he knew he was busted.

"I'm sorry, Nickie," Max said apologetically. "I know I shouldn't have done that."

"I'm sorry, too, honey," answered Nickie. "But I guess this means that you are doing the dishes and walking the dog for the rest of the week."

"Nickie, didn't you see what happened?" Max exclaimed. "That trucker almost killed us!"

"No, Max," she quickly countered. "You almost got us killed by driving angry and pulling a stunt like that in the first place. Now, do you want to add vacuuming to your list this week?"

Nickie was not as calm as she sounded. Enforcing these consequences was no fun for her, either. But she was proud of herself for not giving in or making excuses for Max's behavior. And she was even more confident that she could do this again if she had to.

Now we will go back and break this scenario down so you can see how to design your own.

Time of day: 5:00 pm

Location: driving home on the freeway

People involved: Nickie and Max

Principle violated: Angry driving

What he says and does: He gunned the engine and whipped out of his lane, careening down the shoulder and shooting through a tiny hole next to an 18-wheeler. Then the 18-wheeler moved into the lane, too. Max jammed on his brakes, squealed his tires, shouted a string of obscenities and hit his horn, all in one motion. He knew he was in trouble and tried to apologize.

What you say and do: Nickie said, "I guess this means that you are doing the dishes and walking the dog for the rest of the week." She also said she would require that he do the vacuuming, too, if he didn't cool it.

How you might feel afterward: Nickie was a little shaken up, but proud of herself for sticking to her guns. She was also more confident that she could do it again.

Now, pick a scenario of moderate intensity that is likely to happen in the course of any given day in your relationship with your husband. Visualize how it is likely to begin and play out, filling in all the details below.

MODERATE ANGER SCENARIO

Time of day: _____

Location: _____

People involved: _____

Principle violated: _____

What he says and does: _____

_____

_____

_____

_____

_____

_____

What you will say and do: _____

_____

_____

_____

_____

_____

_____

How you might feel afterward: _____

_____

_____

_____

SEVERE ANGER SCENARIO

If your man becomes abusive and violent during his anger events, then you must be prepared to enforce the consequences you have chosen, should the need arise. This will not be easy or pleasant. But the reason you have come this far in the book is because your life with him so far hasn't been easy or pleasant, and you want that to change. This is a battle you can win, but you must stick to the plan. Study the example below:

Michelle had been so sure Jack was doing better. He was going to that class, he had read the book. She could tell he was trying. But something must have happened at work today. He slammed the door when he got home, and he had shouted at the kids for leaving their toys on the sidewalk. That was two violations in less than two minutes. She knew she was going to have to go back to the bedroom and tell him that he had just earned some consequences. They had just been joking about this last night. Suddenly, it didn't seem so funny.

When she entered the bedroom, he was sitting on the bed, staring out the window. His face was still flushed.

"Sweetheart," she began. "We need to have a talk. You were pretty hard on the kids just then and you know what that means."

"Don't mess with me, Michelle!" Jack snapped as he jumped up from the bed and turned around to face her. "The last thing I need today is some self-righteous baby-sitter telling me what to do."

"Baby, maybe we better take a time out," Michelle offered. "I'll just leave the room until you cool down."

"Don't you walk out on me when I am talking to you, woman!" Jack shouted. "Can't you take a little emotion, a little reality from a real man? I ain't gonna be your lap dog for you to drag around on a chain no more."

"This conversation is over," Michelle said, as she turned and hurried for the door.

"Don't you walk out on me when I am talking to you!" Jack shouted, even louder.

He grabbed her by the arm and jerked her back into the room, catching her face on the side of the door in the process. She tried to push him away, but he spun her around, grabbed her by the hair, and dragged her toward the bed. He would tell the police later that he was just trying to hold her down so he could talk to her. But she bit him on the arm and pulled free. She sprinted through the door and into the living room. The kids were playing in the back yard so she headed for the front door, grabbing the cordless phone off the kitchen counter as she ran by. She pushed 911 as she headed out the door.

Jack saw that she had the phone, so he bolted for the garage, got in the car, and sped away. When the police and the EMS arrived, Michelle provided details of the incident to the police while the paramedics treated the cuts and bruises on her face. She told the police that she wanted to press charges and she wanted Jack arrested. When he tried to sneak back into the house sometime after midnight, the police were waiting for him. They arrested him and took him to jail. Michelle did not answer the phone when Jack called the next morning, and she did not go down and post bail for him.

Michelle was sick at heart. This was a huge setback. But as she went over the events that happened, she knew she had done everything correctly. She could have just ignored his initial outburst, but that would have only led to more and more ugly outbursts. She responded calmly, she asked for a time out, she tried to leave. None of those things helped to shut off the anger. When the violence started she called 911. It had been her only choice. She wasn't glad this had happened, but she was glad she called 911 and she did not regret filing charges. This had to STOP! And she was more determined than ever to not let his anger win.

Obviously this event was more intense, more upsetting. And it requires a much stronger, definite response. If you face such a situation, you must be prepared to follow Michelle's example. Let's summarize it below:

Time of day: Around 6 pm.

Location: at home.

People involved: Michelle and Jack, kids outside in backyard.

Principle violated: yelling, door slamming, non-affectionate touching.

What he says and does: He slammed the door and yelled at the kids. He yelled at her defiantly when she tried to talk to him about his anger. He refused a time out. He grabbed her when she tried to leave and banged her face into the side of the door. He pulled her hair and tried to pin her down on the bed.

What you say and do: Michelle tried to discuss the situation calmly. She asked for a time out and she tried to leave the room. When he became violent, she called 911. When the police came, she filed charges. She did not try to get Jack out of jail.

How you might feel afterward: Michelle was dazed, shaken, discouraged, but still committed to stick to the plan and not let his anger win.

Even though this may be unpleasant to think about, it is very important to plan now what you will say and do if you have to. Visualize a severe anger scenario, maybe a worst-case scenario. Describe it below, and explain how you will respond.

SEVERE ANGER SCENARIO

Time of day: _____

Location: _____

People involved: _____

Principle violated: _____

What he says and does: _____

Chapter 5 • The Line in the Sand

_____
_____
_____
_____
_____
_____

What you will say and do: _____
_____
_____
_____
_____
_____

How you might feel afterward: _____
_____
_____
_____

Be prepared for the battles, because they will come. If you have come this far, you must believe that this relationship is worth fighting for. Here is one important thing to think about: you are not responsible for results; you are only responsible for sticking to the plan. The chances are good that he will begin to change, but how long or how much work it may take is anybody's guess. Don't be discouraged if it goes slowly, and don't blame yourself if it doesn't seem to be coming together the way you expected. You have been blamed for too many things already in this relationship. Leave the blame where it really belongs – at the feet of the guy who needs to control his anger.

A Closing Prayer

If you haven't done so yet, feel free to take a few minutes right now to ask God to help you to make it through this difficult process. If you are not comfortable with praying, that is okay. All you have to do is tell God how you feel and ask for what you need. We don't care what denomination or religion or doctrines you believe or don't believe. Sometimes, it is just important to surrender to a Higher Power and admit that you don't have all the answers yourself. If you need courage or strength, if you are feeling afraid or worried, if you need direction or guidance, just put that in your prayer. Even if you don't know how to say it in a way that looks right to you, God will get the message just the same.

Dear God,

_____

_____

_____

_____

_____

_____

_____

_____

_____

_____

_____

_____

_____

_____

_____   _____
Signed   Date

Chapter 5 • *The Line in the Sand* 175

Announcement Worksheet

Fill in each section below. Be sure to be clear and specific so that your partner will know what you are asking him to do and why.

A. I have decided _____

_____

_____

_____

B. Beginning immediately, I want you to stop the following behaviors:

Behavior to stop: _____

Why it must stop: _____

_____

_____

Behavior to stop: _____

Why it must stop: _____

_____

_____

Behavior to stop: _____

Why it must stop: _____

_____

_____

Behavior to stop: _____

Why it must stop: _____

_____

_____

Behavior to stop: _____

Why it must stop: _____

_____

_____

Behavior to stop:_____

Why it must stop: _____

_____

_____

Behavior to stop:_____

Why it must stop: _____

_____

_____

Behavior to stop:_____

Why it must stop: _____

_____

_____

Behavior to stop:_____

Why it must stop: _____

_____

_____

Behavior to stop:_____

Why it must stop: _____

_____

_____

Behavior to stop:_____

Why it must stop: _____

_____

_____

Chapter 5 • The Line in the Sand

Behavior to stop: _____

Why it must stop: _____

_____

_____

Behavior to stop: _____

Why it must stop: _____

_____

_____

C. What I want you to do next is _____

_____

_____

_____

D. If you do not fully comply with these requests I will _____

_____

_____

_____

_____

_____

Please do not fail to take these requests very seriously, because I am very serious about what I have listed here.

_____   _____

                          Signed   Date

"YOU'VE BEEN ON HOLD FOR OVER AN HOUR... WOULD YOU LIKE US TO PUT YOU IN TOUCH WITH A 'PHONE RAGE' THERAPIST?"

CHAPTER 6
ABCs for Your Own Recovery

Sarah knew it was coming. She just didn't know when. She had been married to Keith for ten years now, and she could read his rage cycle like an airline schedule. It had been eight days since his last really big blow-up. Over the past two years it was rare for him to ever go longer than ten days without some sort of very unpleasant incident. So Sarah was certain that sometime within the next 48 hours, or at the most, 72 hours, he was going to rage again.

The problem was that this was Thursday. That meant Keith would be primed for an attack sometime over the weekend, and her sister and family were planning to be here this weekend. They were all supposed to go to the lake, go water skiing, take the kids to the movies, have a big barbeque, and generally just chill out and have a nice time. That would all be spoiled if Keith kept to his regular cycle. Sarah shuddered at the thought of her husband going into a rage, accusing her and her sister of being something that rhymes with witches, throwing the drink cooler and the seat cushions overboard, and swamping the neighbor kid's jet ski with the wake from the boat right before he rammed into the dock.

There was only one solution; she would have to trigger him early. She had done it before. Actually, she had done it several times. It was never a nice experience, and it could sometimes be a little risky, but it was usually worth the pain and suffering in order to buy a little safety for something more important, Jacob's birthday or Thanksgiving, for instance. Keith was always so nice for about 48 hours after he had a rage attack. He was sweet and he would buy her stuff and agree to pretty much anything she said. Yes, she knew what she had to do.

About that time, she heard Keith pull into the driveway. She decided it had better be tonight, after Jake went to bed. She already knew how to set it up. The bill from Neiman-Marcus came today, the one for the three new outfits and three pairs of shoes that she bought after the big blow-up last month. She was pretty sure that asking Keith to move $1,200 into her account to cover that bill would just about do the trick.

Living with a crazy person can make you crazy. Rageaholics do and say all sorts of wild, crazy, scary and destructive things. If you have survived all these years of living with one, you have been forced to make all sorts of adjustments and choices, and most of them seem pretty crazy to people who haven't walked in your shoes. Who in their right mind would go and pick a fight with a confirmed anger addict, rageaholic wild man? Probably nobody except his wife, who is trading a little pain now for a little peace later. It seems nuts to most people. It makes perfect sense to anyone who has been there.

But just because you have *been* there doesn't mean you have to *stay* there. The whole point of this book is to help couples relocate their marriages and their lives to a safer, saner address. In the last chapter, you worked very hard on a plan to get your husband's attention in order to motivate him to work on his problem. In this chapter, we hope to motivate you to work just that hard on you.

Learning Your ABCs

The first three chapters of this book were designed to teach men how to control their anger by learning a new set of ABCs: Abstain, Believe and Communicate. By stopping certain behaviors, trusting in certain new truths and communicating in ways that are safer and more helpful, anger addicts really can break the power of their anger addiction.

But what about the woman who has been living with him all those years? His anger has had a devastating effect on her. She has been forced to learn a set of survival skills that may have helped to keep her a little safer in the short term. However, over time, the compromises she had to make and the feelings she had to ignore or deny begin to wear away at her ability to act and feel normal. More to the point, her definition of normal gets so distorted that, well ... she forgets how to be her old, normal self. Her home and her marriage aren't normal. What else can you expect?

In this chapter, we will help you learn a new set of ABCs for yourself, following the same pattern used with the men: Abstain, Believe and Communicate. We want to encourage you to stop doing and thinking certain things, start trusting in some new, important truths, and learn to communicate in ways that are safer and more helpful.

Abstain From These Behaviors and Phrases With Your Partners

Women involved with rageaholics resort to all sorts of tactics in an attempt to control the rage attacks. Unfortunately, most of these tactics are verbal, which gives the rager just one more excuse to get worked up in an argument. The result, then, of most of these tactics is to increase or intensify arguments. They don't resolve anything and can generally make things worse.

The wording of the phrases can vary widely, but the core strategies generally fall into just a handful of categories:

Reasoning – You just want to talk to him and encourage him to process his feeling more rationally and calmly.

Confronting – No more Mrs. Nice Lady. Let's see how he likes it when I get tough.

Accusing – This category can also take several forms, but the idea is to use shame or blame or humiliation to manipulate him into changing. No matter what the message is, the goal is to "guilt-trip" him into doing better. (Just FYI, no matter what he says to you, he is already feeling guilty. Piling on more guilt just makes him feel more trapped, which produces more anger.)

Threatening – When all else fails, use threats. Threatening isn't always bad, but never make a threat that you aren't absolutely ready and willing to carry out. Using threats in the middle of an argument is a recipe for disaster.

Below are 11 phrases that we are strongly encouraging you to stop using with your partner. They don't help, and they can make things worse. They each fit into at least one of the four categories we mentioned above. As you study each one, try to guess which unhelpful category it fits in, and record the appropriate letter in the blank next to it.

R = REASONING
C = CONFRONTING
A = ACCUSING
T = THREATENING

1. "GO AHEAD AND TELL ME HOW YOU REALLY FEEL." _____

Anger addicts thrive on expressing feelings, mostly angry ones. Expressing anger charges their anger batteries and increases the intensity of their anger event. If he is working on this Anger Busting program, too, then his assignment is to *avoid speaking* when angry. Don't try to draw him out. It would be better to let the moment pass without saying anything. Tomorrow, tell him "thank you" for restraining himself.

2. "TELL ME WHEN YOU ARE ANGRY. DON'T LET IT BUILD UP." _____

It might seem logical to let anger out before it builds to a boiling point. But with an addict, letting out his anger is one of the things that *causes* it to build to a boiling point. If he takes the lid off, he will boil over. He must turn the fire down. That means not discussing his anger at all while he is angry. The anger will then gradually weaken and cool down.

3. "WE NEED TO RESOLVE THIS RIGHT **NOW!**" _____

This kind of a demand is usually secret code for, "I know I am right and I am going to make us go over it and over and over it until you give in and agree with me!" This is not a very good technique for solving problems in any relationship, but it is a terrible way to talk to an anger addict. It might be better for you to take a few minutes each, spread over several evenings, to gradually express your opinions. Make allowances for time outs and don't press for an immediate solution. He is not only trying to listen to you, he is trying to cool down his anger.

4. "You are always running away. You never want to talk with me." _____

It is **always** better for a rageaholic to end the conversation and leave the room before he has an anger attack. And if he feels that he is being criticized for something, or asked to fix a problem that seems hopeless at the moment, that will trigger a feeling of being trapped. Situations like this stoke the fire on his anger. If he needs to leave or take a time out, this is not bad. Talk later, when things are safer.

5. "If you are going to scream at me, then I am going to scream at you." _____

Another great way to escalate an anger event. Instead, try saying, "Please lower your voice." If that doesn't work, simply tell him you won't discuss things if he is going to yell.

6. "You are sick and you will never get better. Men like you only get worse over time." _____

Sadly, this is sometimes true, *but it is not always true.* And if you truly want to encourage him to try and get better, this is not a good way to start. Give him a copy of this workbook, or give him the name of a counselor. Ask for a trial separation while he works on his anger. Don't tell him he is hopeless. If you believe he really is hopeless, then leave; don't stick around and tell him about it over and over again.

7. "How can you say that you love me when you treat me like that?" _____

The problem isn't love, the problem is anger. He doesn't rage because he doesn't love you, he rages because he has an anger addiction. Don't talk about love, talk about getting anger under control. He would much rather fill your head with all sorts of mushy talk about how much he cares for you and how sorry he is, but that is a dead end. Instead, ask him what he is going to do differently so that you don't divorce him.

8. "Go ahead and hit me. I know that's what you really want to do." _____

Maybe you want to show him you are tough and won't be intimidated. But using this phrase could definitely take you places you don't want to go. If you want to shut down his anger, don't say anything at all. Silence in the face of a potential anger incident is the most effective weapon you have.

9. "You're crazy. The things you get jealous over make no sense at all." _____

Rageaholics very often do have a problem with jealousy. Deep-seated insecurities and the fear of abandonment make them extremely dependent on the women in their lives which, in turn, leads them to jealousy. He doesn't like it, either. In fact, he even feels a little crazy himself. When you sense that he feels jealous over something, try asking him what you could do to help him get over it. Assure him that you love him and he is the only man for you.

10. "THIS IS IT! I AM GOING TO DIVORCE YOU THIS TIME. NO ONE IS GOING TO TALK TO ME LIKE THAT." _____

Sometimes divorce is unavoidable, even necessary. But threatening divorce during an argument is almost certain to add fuel to the fire and make his anger worse. It will not calm him down or bring him to his senses. Instead, call a time out. When he has calmed down, tell him how his angry outburst made you feel and ask him what he intends to do to make it up to you.

11. "YOU WILL NEVER GET ANY BETTER UNTIL YOU GO TO THERAPY AND WORK THROUGH YOUR ISSUES WITH YOUR FATHER. THAT'S WHAT MY THERAPIST SAID IS WRONG WITH YOU." _____

First of all, telling your husband that you and your counselor have been talking about him, analyzing him behind his back, and blaming him for all the problems in the marriage is a great way to start another argument. Besides that, angry men *can* get their anger under control without spending months or years in therapy. Urge him to read this book, see a therapist and do this program if you think he needs help. Don't use psychological doubletalk in hopes of manipulating him or shaming him.

AND THE ANSWER IS

Some of these statements could fit into more than one category, so there isn't a set of absolute right answers here. The idea is for you to review these phrases and avoid using them, or anything that sounds or feels like them. But just for the record, we labeled the phrases as follows.

1. R	7. A
2. R	8. C
3. C	9. A
4. C	10. T
5. C	11. A
6. A	

DOES THE SHOE FIT?

Did you see yourself anywhere in these questions or strategies? We are not trying to criticize you or make you feel bad. But it is important to recognize what is not working so that you can move on to something that will. There is an old phrase in the addiction recovery movement that goes like this: *"The more you do what you always did, the more you will get what you always got."* That just makes sense, doesn't it? Are you tired of getting what you always got? Then it is time to stop doing what you always did.

Testing Your Communication Tendencies

Read over the scenario below. Then choose the answer that best describes how you would normally respond to a similar situation in your own marriage.

Jesse stormed into the bedroom the minute Marta hung up the phone. She had been talking to her mom, just getting caught up on family events over the past week.

"I hate it; I just hate it when you do that!" snarled Jesse.

"Hate what?" stammered Marta. She wasn't surprised that he was angry. But she honestly had no clue what it was about this time.

*"I hate the way you blab all of our business to your family," Jesse snapped. "You had **no right** to tell your mom that my hours got cut back at work this week."*

*Jesse's tone was starting to get really out of control now. "It's just temporary anyhow. But now she is going to freak out and think I can't support you and start talking bad about me. **You had no right!**"*

And with that, he grabbed a coffee cup off of the night stand, hurled it across the room, and smashed it into the wall.

Now, circle the number of the answer below that is the most like the response which, in the past, you would usually make, if you were in Marta's shoes.

1. "Jesse, why don't you try to calm down. This isn't really that big a deal. My mom doesn't hate you. Why don't we go sit down on the couch and talk this out?"

2. "Jesse, you big baby. That was my favorite coffee mug. All you do is yell and break stuff. Can't you think of anybody but yourself?"

3. Saying nothing, you carefully step over the broken shards and walk out of the room.

4. "I swear to you, Jesse, if you do something like that one more time, I am packing my bags and moving in with my sister."

5. "Jesse, your anger is out of control. We can't talk about this tonight."

6. "So, I guess throwing stuff and breaking stuff is the way to win. Well, you better duck." And then you pick up the clock radio from his side of the bed and smash it against the side of the armoire.

Now, if you circled any answer besides #3 or #5, your typical way of dealing with his anger is likely to make things even worse, whether you realize it or not. The other answers correspond to the four basic patterns we talked about earlier.

> Question 1 was Reasoning
> Question 2 was Accusing
> Question 4 was Threatening
> Question 6 was Confronting

After working through the material up to this point, can you guess what patterns you use most often when dealing with your husband's anger? Fill in the blanks below, using either:

>Reasoning
>Accusing
>Threatening
>Confronting

Based on what I have learned here, most of the time I try to cope with my partner's anger style by _____. In very tense situations, I may also try _____ _____.

Now that you have a little better idea of what you have always done, let's move on and learn how to do something different.

WHAT YOU *BELIEVE* DETERMINES WHAT YOU DO

Take a long hard look at this statement:

*Situations don't cause emotions. What we **believe** about the situation is what causes our emotions.*

Go back and read it one more time. Read it out loud. Think about it for just a minute. Now, read it again.

This statement is really true. And what's more, it is usually our *emotional response* to a situation that dictates our *actions*. And that is where we start to get in trouble. Here is a simple example of a belief that can lead to a very sad outcome in some people's lives.

>Belief: People who make bad grades in high school will fail in life.
>Emotion: Since I made bad grades in school, I feel ashamed and hopeless.
>Action: Because I believe I am a failure, and because I am ashamed, I settle for a bad job in a dead end career and jump into a bad marriage.

But, did you know that Albert Einstein — generally believed to be the greatest and smartest physicist of the 20th Century — failed out of high school and came close to not ever going to college? But he knew the *situation* did not have the power to ruin his life. He *believed he could succeed* even though school was hard for him. He didn't give up on himself and he did go to college. He ended up making discoveries that literally changed the world. Where would our world be today if it were *really* true that people who make bad grades in high school will fail in life? Where would we be if Einstein believed he was doomed to fail in life? **Einstein believed something else,** and that made all the difference.

Women in abusive relationships have developed a set of beliefs along the way that are not helpful and not healthy because they are not true. Sometimes they believe they are helpless and have no options to make themselves and their marriages safer. Sometimes they try things that seem to make sense at the time, but just turn out to be wrong. In this section, we will offer you a set of new beliefs, and help you learn to trust them.

BELIEFS FOR WOMEN WHO LOVE ANGRY MEN

Here are a set of nine important principles that can revolutionize the way you function in your marriage, if you will only give them a try.

1. "THERE IS NOTHING WRONG WITH MY GETTING HIM TO CHANGE."

As incredible as this may seem to you at the moment, there is a very good chance that your husband would be willing to change if he had a clear understanding of exactly what you wanted him to do. Remember, anger addicts have a problem with *anger*, not love. He may really love you, but during the anger events, you don't exchange helpful information, you accuse each other and criticize each other. This leaves scars and creates mountains of misunderstanding. He would do a lot better at being the husband you want and need, if you would just *tell him what you want and need*. Instead of sitting there wishing he could read your mind and magically start doing things that would be more helpful, go ahead and spell it out for him. Guys thrive on good instructions and checklists.

2. "THERE IS NOTHING WRONG WITH HIS WANTING TO CHANGE TO PLEASE ME."

Women often recoil at the suggestion that they should tell their husbands what they want and need in very clear terms. A common response is, "I don't want to tell him what to do. It makes me feel like I am his mother. I want him to change because it is his idea, not mine. I want him to change because he loves me, not because he has to." Ladies, it is precisely because he loves you that he can be motivated to change. *You are his reason for wanting to change.* In order to get where he honestly wants to go, he needs good information from you.

3. "IT'S BETTER TO FIGURE OUT THE SOLUTION THAN TO FIGURE OUT THE CAUSE."

Don't waste time analyzing the root causes of your husband's behavior. Even if he recognized and admitted them, it probably won't help control his anger. When the stove catches fire, you can either analyze the drippings in the grease trap, or you can grab the fire extinguisher. What makes more sense to you?

4. "THERE IS A BETTER WAY TO CHANGE THE RELATIONSHIP THAN 'TALKING THINGS OUT.'"

Men are not mentally wired to enjoy talking about needs and feelings the way women are. It may make sense to you to just sit down and talk things out, but it can be very unnerving for men, especially for anger addicts. The stress can actually set up an anger attack. It is better to focus on changing behavior. Instead of asking, "Honey, can we talk about why you did this thing that upset me?" it would be better to say, "Honey, don't do that again. Next time do this instead."

5. "LOVE AND TRUST ARE TWO SEPARATE THINGS."

Addicts are worthy of love, just as all of God's children are. But addicts have big problems with impulse control. It is not unloving to be unwilling to trust them in certain situations. Anger addicts can be repentant, charming, endearing, sweet and kind. They can also snap and rage in hurtful ways. It is okay to say, "Sweetheart, I do love you. But I am not relaxing the boundaries on our relationship until I am absolutely convinced that you have your anger completely under control."

6. "I HAVE COMPLETE TRUST IN MY ABILITY TO TAKE ACTION WHEN NEEDED."

You have worked very hard developing a plan for what to do if he fails to comply with the rules you have set down. Don't focus so much on whether or not he is changing fast enough. Instead, stay committed to your plan. It is a good one and it has the power to make a difference, if you just stick to it.

7. "A LITTLE PSYCHOLOGICAL PAIN CAN BE A GOOD THING."

Really! Don't be so worried about hurting your husband's feelings when you enforce consequences that he finds unpleasant. Remember all the pain and suffering he has put you through? Besides, negative consequences can be a most effective teacher. He won't know that you are really serious – and he probably won't be definitely motivated to pursue change on his own – unless you are willing to let him suffer the consequences of his actions.

8. "PRAISE CAN ONLY HELP."

Perhaps this sounds strange. After all, so much of your relationship has been based on conflict and fear. And the recovery plan is based on very firm, unpleasant consequences. Where does praise fit into all of this? Simple – as he is trying to dig out from all the years of doing things wrong, it gives him a big boost if you can catch him doing something right. Men, even anger addicts, are inspired to try harder and do better when they receive praise and recognition for getting things right. Don't just punish him when he violates the rules; reward him, in small but clear ways, when he succeeds. It will make a big difference.

9. "YOU'VE GOT TO 'KNOW WHEN TO HOLD 'EM, KNOW WHEN TO FOLD 'EM ...'"

In this workbook, we have given you a lot of reasons to hope. Many rageaholics can change and many marriages can be saved, probably more than anybody realizes. But not all men can or will change and not all marriages can be saved. In the final analysis, this is not about whether or not you can change him, it is about whether or not he is willing to change. Sometimes the damage has been too great. Sometimes you are just married to a Cobra who is not designed to function like normal people in the first place. Once you have worked your plan and done all you know to do, if you still do not feel safe and he has indicated no sincere willingness to become a safe person in your life, cash in your chips and move on. You are not a failure if your plan fails or your marriage fails. It is a very wise woman who is willing to choose health, safety, and the possibility of a brighter future somewhere else over continuing to get what she has always gotten.

DOES ANY OF THIS MAKE SENSE TO YOU?

Take a moment to review these nine principles. Slowly read them out loud to yourself, and listen to the words and thoughts as they come out of your mouth.

1. "There is nothing wrong with my getting him to change."
2. "There is nothing wrong with his wanting to change to please me."
3. "It's better to figure out the solution than to figure out the cause."
4. "There is a better way to change the relationship than 'talking things out.'"
5. "Love and trust are two separate things."
6. "I have complete trust in my ability to take action when needed."
7. "A little psychological pain can be a good thing."
8. "Praise can only help"
9. "You've got to 'know when to hold 'em, know when to fold 'em … '"

As you think about each of these ideas, which ones make the most sense to you? Are there any that sound too risky or too strange for you to try? In the blanks below write out the three principles that make the most sense to you, the ones that you would be willing to apply in your own life if you aren't already. And then explain why you think these ideas are worth trying.

The statement _____

makes sense to me, because _____

_____

_____

_____

The statement _____

makes sense to me, because _____

_____

_____

_____

The statement _____

makes sense to me, because _____

_____

_____

_____

Go back over the list one more time and identify the idea that is hardest for you to accept in your situation. Write it in the space below, and explain why you think it might be too hard or might not help.

The principle that seems hardest for me to accept is _____
_____
_____

I'm not sure it would work for me because _____
_____
_____

How would that work for me?

Pick one of the three principles that you found most appealing, and give some thought to how you would apply it at home in your everyday relationship with your partner. Envision yourself making choices based on this new principle. Describe how you might feel and think while implementing this new idea. For example:

Jennifer and Todd had been doing pretty good lately. He had been going to his group every week, and his behavior around her and the kids was really beginning to improve. He was still sleeping at Rick's house, but he came by for supper every night and helped the kids with their homework. They had even been intimate once, and she didn't feel wrong about that. But now he was pressuring her to let him move back in.

"C'mon, Jen," Rick pleaded. "It's been eight weeks now. Don't tell me you can't tell that I am doing better, especially not after Tuesday night. You know I can do this. I know I can do this. Don't you think it's time to call this whole thing off and get back to normal?"

Oooo. It was the thought of "getting back to normal" that brought Jen up hard. She did not want to go back to "normal" ever again. Todd was certainly doing better, and she wanted to reward him somehow. But in her heart she just felt a though it was too soon. The fact that he was pushing for it only confirmed her fear that he was still too unstable. In the past he could charm her or play on her sympathy and get her to drop her guard, but not any more. She loved him, and she was hopeful. But she did not trust him yet. And she had to tell him so.

"Todd, you don't know how hard it is on me and the kids for us to be away from you, too," she explained. "I can tell that you are doing better and I'm really proud of you. But, honey, it is still too early. I'm very uncomfortable with the pressure you're putting on me and that makes me afraid that you haven't made as much progress as you think you have. I definitely love you, but I don't trust that you're ready to make this big step yet. Please don't bring it up again. I will let you know when I am ready."

This scenario breaks down as follows:

Issue: Todd wants to move back home

Summary of events: He tried to convince Jennifer that he had made progress and he was ready to get back to normal. She still felt very uncomfortable.

Her response: She told Todd she loved him but the answer was still no, at least not yet. She loved him but she was not ready to trust him.

Principle applied: Love and trust are two separate things.

Jennifer probably felt: A little sad, a little relieved, and a little proud of herself for sticking to her plan.

Now, use the space below to describe a possible situation where you could apply one of the new principles that is most appealing to you.

Issue: _____

Summary of the way events might develop: _____

_____

_____

_____

_____

_____

Your response: _____

_____

_____

_____

Principle you applied: _____

How you might feel afterward: _____

_____

_____

_____

Chapter 6 • ABCs for Your Own Recovery

A WORD ABOUT YOUR SPIRITUAL BELIEF SYSTEM

You may have a spiritual tradition that encourages wives to submit to and respect their husbands. The Bible mentions this in the book of Ephesians in the New Testament, chapter 5, verse 22. Because of your strong desire to honor God according to your spiritual tradition, some of the ideas we have been discussing in this workbook may seem very uncomfortable to you. Please be assured that we are not suggesting that you do anything that would contradict your spiritual belief system. However, we would like to point out that the Bible has a lot to say about the way husbands are supposed to love their wives, and the way that people are supposed to love each other. Jesus even mentions that we must love others the way we love ourselves, which implies that we must be able to treat ourselves in ways that are loving and safe before we can truly love others.

Please do not try to make what could be a life and death decision on the basis of only one verse. Carefully consider everything the Bible has to say on the subject of love and relationships. Then, try to make a plan that will be the most loving thing you can do for yourself, your kids and your husband. It is not unloving or even disrespectful to create a short-term level of discomfort for your husband if it will result in his learning a better and safer way to live. When you think about it, nothing could be more loving and respectful than that.

COMMUNICATE THESE PRINCIPLES IN YOUR DAILY CONVERSATION

For most of your relationship with the angry man in your life, things have been pretty complicated. You have spent lots of time trying to figure out what to say and what not to say, hoping to avoid triggering his anger. You have tried to walk on eggshells, hoping to keep from being a target. You have begged and pleaded, and done your share of yelling and screaming and as well. Even after all these years, you are no closer to really knowing what to do.

Until now. We hope this workbook is helping you to feel more confident about what to do, and more hopeful about your future. We want to close this section by giving you a handful of ideas to focus on as you communicate with your husband every day. Think of this as your little Swiss Army knife, to replace that old tool box full of coping ideas and attitudes that really didn't work anyway.

COMMUNICATE WITH A K.I.S.S.

K.I.S.S. stands for keep it sweet and simple. Here are seven clear, simple principles to focus on during discussions with your husband.

1. MONITOR THE PROGRESS. INSIST ON A SOFT VOLUME AND A NICE TONE.

This is more about the emotions than the content of your conversations. You may have an honest disagreement going, and it may be unclear who is really right and who is wrong. But that is not the problem. The issue is anger, and whenever the tone starts to get angry, that is where the trouble starts. Interrupt your husband immediately whenever he starts to sound loud or mean. Simply point it out by saying, in a very calm voice, "Honey, your voice is starting to sound loud and mean." If he doesn't get it under control, end the conversation.

2. BE READY TO END THE CONVERSATION.

Once the conversation turns angry, you are headed for trouble. Be ready to end the conversation immediately. Just say, "This conversation is over. Maybe we can try again tomorrow." Leave the room if you need to. Don't let him bait you into continuing past the point when you know it is going the wrong way.

3. DON'T EXPECT HIM TO BRING UP MAJOR ISSUES.

Most men are not mentally oriented to explore the deep complexities of life and relationships. They can be trained to do it, but they aren't naturally inclined to do it. Don't take it personally when they seem to be ignoring things that are important to you. A guy tends to function in marriage pretty much as he functions at work. Unless the boss changes the job description, he assumes that everything must be okay. So, if you have things that you want to bring up, *go ahead and bring them up*. As long as you do it in a way that doesn't accuse him of being a failure, he will probably listen and he might even appreciate the information.

4. POINT OUT IN A SOFT TONE WHEN HE IS NOT FOLLOWING HIS ABSTINENCE PROGRAM, OR WHEN YOU HAVEN'T HEARD A COMPLIMENT IN A FEW DAYS.

His part of the program is to work on changing. Your part of the program is to keep him accountable by enforcing boundaries. Instead of getting your feelings hurt and clamming up when he breaks a rule, quietly but firmly point it out to him. Don't ask him to explain. *Just tell him to get back in the game*. And don't be afraid to ask him to make it up to you somehow.

5. BETTER TO SAY WHAT YOU WANT THAN ASK WHAT HE FEELS.

Women talk about feelings, men talk about football. He needs information from you in order to know what he can do that would help you the most. Just tell him.

6. CATCH HIM DOING SOMETHING RIGHT.

See if you can overdo compliments in appropriate situations. Nothing makes a guy feel like King of the World more than hearing his wife say, "I am so proud of you. Thank you for all your hard work. I am so glad you are in my life." He will try even harder next time.

7. LIVE IN "BEHAVIOR LAND," NOT "PSYCHOLOGY LAND."

The world of psychoanalysis and therapy is a very subjective, personal environment. Each person is different—different history, different memories, different emotional needs to meet and wounds to heal. No one can go there for someone else, and you can't take someone there unless they want to go. There is a time and place for that stuff, but you don't need to take your husband there to have a better marriage. Focus on behavior, not feelings, and focus on now, not the past. Tell what you need and ask for what you want in behavioral terms. What do you want him to *do*? Tell him that, and he will already be on his way to helping to make the marriage better for both of you.

PRACTICE MAKES IT MORE LIKELY THAT YOU CAN DO IT WHEN YOU REALLY NEED TO.

Below you will find a series of phrases that are keyed to the communication principles that we discussed above. Under each phrase is a set of blanks. In these blanks, describe the typical situations or issues in your marriage where these phrases could come in handy. For example:

"Baby, thanks so much for your hard work. I am so proud of you."

Uses:

When he stops himself before getting angry.

When he goes out of his way to help with the kids.

When he completes a project around the house that you have been asking for.

Now it's your turn.

Strategic Phrase: *"Your voice is getting louder and you are talking mean."*

Uses: _____

_____

_____

_____

Strategic Phrase: *"I'm sorry, but I am not going to have this conversation now. Maybe we can talk about it again tomorrow."*

Uses: _____

_____

_____

_____

Strategic Phrase: *"Honey, do you have a couple of minutes for me to share some things with you that I need help with?"*

Uses: _____

_____

_____

_____

Strategic Phrase: *"You promised that you would not (fill in the blank with the banned behavior he has just violated). I am very serious about your need to abstain from that. What are you going to do to make it up to me?"*

Uses: _____

_____

_____

_____

Strategic Phrase: *"Here is what you could do right now that would help me the most."*

Uses: _____

_____

_____

_____

Strategic Phrase: *"Baby, thanks so much for your hard work. I am so proud of you."*

Uses: _____

_____

_____

_____

Strategic Phrase: *"Sweetheart, I want you to know that if you will just do these things we have talked about today, it will make me really happy and proud to be your wife."*

Uses: _____

_____

_____

_____

Now that you have found some practical uses for these phrases, use them! Begin by going back and reading each phrase out loud several times. Listen to your voice saying them. Get used to the idea of communicating with your partner in these terms. And do it often. You will both notice a big difference.

DON' FORGET:

Recovery from addictions is a process, not an event. People don't change overnight—not your husband and not you either. It is going to take time and hard work from both of you for your marriage to reach a new, better, safer level. This workbook provides a good road map, and you have already done some good work. But you still might need the help of a capable therapist to refine your insights and help you make hard decisions. Anger addicts can get better. Wives can learn how to make healthier choices. Marriages can be saved. Work your plan and give it time to work. And giving it a little prayer couldn't hurt either. You aren't in charge of results. You are only in charge of doing your best. If you do that, you will be a success, no matter what happens next.

"I'm competitive, cruel, glad when my friends fail—and so envious when they succeed that I wish them nothing but evil. Other than that, I've no idea why I'm here."

Epilogue

"Be angry; just don't sin. Instead of avoiding the problem, deal with your anger now, before the sun goes down! If you face your anger now, the Adversary won't have an opportunity to make your life miserable later." – New Testament, Ephesians 4:26-27 (paraphrased)

Isn't it interesting that the Bible doesn't tell us that anger is bad, or that we should stuff it or ignore it? The Bible doesn't say anger is wrong, it just says there is a right way and a wrong way to deal with it. If you choose the wrong way, chaos and disaster will result. Apparently, the most important thing to do is face it *now*, and choose wisely, before things get worse.

Please remember, conquering anger addiction — like conquering any other addiction — requires lots of courage, honesty, hard work and patience. If you are an addict, expect this to be the fight of your life; probably the fight *for* your life. Embrace the Anger Busting principles and let them become a part of who you are. You will continue to have slips, but you will also begin to have more wins. Over time, the way you think and feel and choose will begin to change. Will you ever be completely free of this struggle? Probably not. Can you learn to control this anger so that it doesn't continue to hurt you and those around you? Absolutely.

Living with an anger addict takes every bit as much courage, honesty, hard work and patience. If that is where you are today, please try to have realistic expectations. The addict in your life is going to slip, in spite of the fact that he may be sincerely and faithfully following the program. When this happens, it might not be the end of the world or the end of the relationship. Just hang in there and don't be afraid to follow through on your part of the program. If he gets up and gets back in the game without blaming you or anyone else, that would be a very good sign. Only time will tell.

As you put this workbook down and get ready to work out the principles in your life, take a moment to soak in the wisdom of this old American Indian fable:

Two Wolves

A young Native American boy sought comfort from his grandfather after being unfairly treated by the older boys in the village. The lad was hurt, confused, and very angry. He was spoiling for a fight.

"Young One, I too have experienced these feelings many times," the old man said. " I have seen much sadness and felt many cuts in my heart over many years. So often it has felt like two strong wolves were fighting to be the Great Chief of my spirit."

"What were they fighting about, Grandfather?" inquired the boy.

"It seems to me that one wolf is good," he replied. "He is wise and strong and tries to see past the hurt and look for ways to heal."

A look of profound sadness momentarily clouded his eyes. He seemed to shudder slightly as he pulled his blanket more tightly around his shoulders.

"But he is fighting against a very ferocious warrior." Grandfather's voice was distant and wistful, as if he wasn't really talking to the boy anymore at all. "That other wolf is so angry, so bitter and vengeful. He seems to want only to deal out pain and destruction until his appetite for rage is fully satisfied."

He turned his attention once more to the boy.

"The battle between these two wolves is always fierce," the grandfather explained. "And it is a fight to the death."

With a wide-eyed and worried look, the boy exclaimed, "Oh, Grandfather, which one will win?"

Grandfather let out a long, wistful sigh and simply said, "The one I feed, young one. The one I feed."

Bon appetit!

Appendix

Leading Involuntary Anger Management Groups

Many men with anger problems find themselves mandated to participate in an anger management group. If you've been sent to a group, or if you are leading such a group, here are some thoughts. The following guidelines were adapted from a portion of Newton Hightower's Certification Training Program for Anger Resolution Therapy™.

Context for Involuntary Anger Management Groups:

Most of the people in the group do not come because they think they have an anger problem. They are there because someone else, someone who has the power to enforce their being there, thinks they have an anger problem.

Purpose for Involuntary Anger Management Groups:

- For the members to be aware of the many ways they express their anger... both by looking back into the recent past and in the present.

- For the members to be aware that many times they feel anger and do not express it.

- For members to get clear about how to keep from expressing anger when they feel it.

- For members to imagine scenes in the future and see themselves doing something positive.

- For members to adopt the goal of having anger and not expressing it… to improve impulse control. A = Abstain

- For members to see that sometimes you can win by losing. They can learn to lose without suffering humiliation. B = Believe

- For members to learn to get their ego out of arguments by learning to say the words "You are right. I am sorry. I was wrong" convincingly, without experiencing humiliation and shame. C = Communicate

METHOD FOR INVOLUNTARY ANGER MANAGEMENT GROUPS:

Awareness and Impulse Control are not learned in a textbook. The best way to improve anger control is through awareness, i.e., by becoming aware of how the anger process works, and then by abstaining from the expression of anger. Most of the people in the groups have used up their right to express their anger for the rest of their lives. They have abused the privilege and need to turn in the privilege.

Many therapists suffer from depression, low self-esteem and the inability to express anger. They have gone to therapy to learn to get in touch with their anger, express it appropriately and ask for what they want.

If that is your history, do not project your personality on anger addicts!

Rest assured of this: anger addicts are different. Their problem is not the same as your problem. Anger addicts have never had a problem standing up for their "rights" or "expressing themselves." Most of them have had a life-long problem shutting up, as well as a life-long problem of thinking they are entitled to have their way. Most of the people in your anger management group will be narcissistic, selfish, self-centered and self-absorbed with a streak of anti-social personality disorder. Anger addicts have narcissistic personality disorders, with poor impulse control. Angry men consistently test higher than average on self-esteem.

If you are going to lead an effective group, burn the following set of goals into your brain:

What My Goal Is NOT:

- My goal is not to be nice to these clients, to make up for the mean treatment they received as children.

- My goal is not to avoid making them angry with me.

- My goal is not to "work through" their issues.

- My goal is not to increase their awareness of their sexism.

- My goal is not to help them get in touch with their other feelings.

- My goal is not to help them to express their anger appropriately.
- My goal is not to help them learn about new ways to express their anger.

GROUP SESSION 1:

Going over the rules...

1. Introduce yourself and welcome them to the class. Ignore all the initial sarcastic remarks and questions.

2. Go over the rules. Make them crystal clear and never bend them in the slightest way for any reason... no matter what! Otherwise, I promise you chaos.

3. Rules must fit the setting you are in, and have consequences. In a therapeutic community, the rules of the community will still apply. Whatever the consequences are for throwing chairs and screaming should be applied.

4. Here are rules that work well with Court Ordered Outpatient Domestic Violence Offenders Groups (ongoing: meaning people came in and out after they finished their required number of sessions in the required time).

    - This group will meet every Tuesday night from 6:00 pm until 7:30 pm.

    - You must attend ten sessions out of the next twelve to get your letter of completion for your probation officer.

    - If you are more than ten minutes late, your attendance is not counted. That is by my watch. Feel free to synchronize your watch with mine. You are free to come late. You will not be charged, but it won't count toward your 10 session in 12 weeks.

    - If you leave before 7:30 pm, your attendance will not be counted... that means by *my watch*.

    - You must pay all your fees before I will send a letter of verification of any kind to your probation officer. Some of your POs will want verification every week. I will provide that as long as your fees are paid. No money? No letter.

    - The only things the letter will say is that you came, were cooperative, applied the techniques we discussed and successfully completed the anger management course.

    - Some of you may want me to evaluate whether you are better or worse. I will not put one single word of evaluation in the letter. This is a class for people with anger problems. I know how to teach people to get over that problem, but I don't know how to predict the future.

- Most POs will be happy with that kind of letter, but if they want an evaluation, then show them this list of rules.

- No cold beer before you come here. No drugs or alcohol of any kind before you come. If you show up even the slightest bit intoxicated, then I will ask you to leave and I will report it to your PO. If you don't leave when I ask you to, I will call the police.

After explaining the rules, ask for questions. Do not spend more than two minutes answering questions.

1. Do not answer "why" questions. "Why" questions are invitations for arguments. Before the course is over, you may have a chance to teach them that. Do not explain why you do not answer why questions. Just don't answer them.

    Possible responses to "why" questions:

    - "Good question. I don't know why I have that rule. Other questions?"

    - "You are right. That probably would be more fair, but I like being unfair sometimes, so I am going to keep the rule."

    - "The only 'why' question you will ever answer is why you do this work. Best answer: "Easy money. I have boat payments to make. We are both slaves of the probation department. I need the money, and you need the letter."

2. Agree to every negative about you. "Yeah, you are right. I am mean and unreasonable sometimes."

3. Do not bend to their excuses. If they say they cannot comply with one of the rules, like: "There is no way I can be here on time every week!" then very softly and politely suggest that they check back with their probation officer. Perhaps they can find another class that doesn't meet at this time. Tell them they are free to leave now if they like… no charge for today. You will be surprised how suddenly a lot of them can get there by 6:00 pm.

4. Do not try to be their friend. If they ask if you care about them: "Care about you? Why should I care about you? I don't even know you."

Group Building Exercise: This game makes it clear, without you saying it, that the members will participate. It also shows that you are a warm and friendly person… just inflexible about the rules and unwilling to explain yourself in any way.

Therapist: *Okay, we're going to start with an exercise. The way this exercise works is the person on my left is going to say his name and what city and state he was born in. Then the next man will repeat the first man's first and last name, and the city and state he was born in, followed by his own. The next man will repeat the first two and add his own, etc., until it comes around to me and I have to repeat them all... or try to, at least. Okay, start if off.*

Joe: Do I have to do this? I don't want to.

Therapist: (big smile) Yeah, you have to. It's part of the torture.

Joe: I have had enough torture. Just getting arrested was enough torture. I mean I wasn't doing anything...

Therapist: (interrupting... You will do it a hundred times. Insist on interrupting. They are to practice silence when interrupted. If they challenge you, keep talking louder. "Hey, your job is to be quiet when I interrupt you.") Joe... first and last name. I don't want the story of your life, just first and last name, then city and state.

Joe: I thought this was group therapy and I could say what I want.

Therapist: This ain't Bob Newhart. You are on probation for domestic violence, trying to get a letter saying you cooperated in the class. Joe... get back to reality... your first and last name, city and state.

Joe: That's just it. I shouldn't be on probation.

Therapist: Joe, this is the first principle you need to learn: SILENCE. Now the next time you open your mouth, it should be with your first and last name, city and state where you were born, or I will give you a last name, city and state where you were born.

Joe: Go ahead.

Therapist: Okay. This is Joe Runs-His-Mouth from Muleshoe, Texas. I hope this gets easier or I am going to ask for a raise.

Bill: (second man) I am Bill Dartmore. I was born in Dalhart, Texas.

Therapist: First give Joe's first and last name, and where he was born, then yours.

Bill: Oh, sorry.

Therapist: No problem. I forgot the rules myself before I got through with Joe Runs-His-Mouth, from Muleshoe, Texas.

Bill: This is Joe Runs-His-Mouth from Muleshoe, Texas. I am Bill Dartmore and I was born in Dalhart, Texas.

Randy: I don't get the point of this.

Therapist: That's good. Your first and last name and city and state you were born.

Randy: You mean you don't care that I don't understand?

Therapist:	Name please. I am going to need anger management by the time we get around the circle. Maybe probation can find me an easier group. This is too much trouble for what they are paying me. (The client should suffer. The therapist should not suffer, or at least not more than the client. So far, they are winning. Time to raise the ante. Retorts will be a little stronger from now on.)
Randy:	Randy Duncan. I was born in Dallas, Texas.
Therapist:	Start with the first man. I am going to require an I.Q. test before we start next week. This whole group must have brain damage or Alzheimer's.
Randy:	I forgot.
Therapist:	He is Joe Runs-His-Mouth, born in Muleshoe, Texas.
Joe:	Actually, I am Joe Robinson, born in Chicago, Illinois.
Therapist:	Oh, no! Now you are confusing us! (Fake misery. Laughter.) Okay Randy. What is Joe's name and where was he born?
Randy:	His name is Joe Robinson, born in Chicago, Illinois. His name is Bill Dartmore. I don't remember where he was born.
Therapist:	Tell him Bill.
Bill:	Dalhart, Texas.
Therapist:	Now your name.
Randy:	I am Randy Duncan, born in Dallas, Texas.

The purpose of that exercise was to establish:

- That you are running the group.
- This is not a discussion or process group... more of a class.
- We are playing by your rules.
- You are not going to get into explaining and arguing.
- You are willing to get as tough as needed to get appropriate participation.
- You preferred to make things fun and have a good time.
- When it came your time, you were going to participate in the group activities as well... not likely you are going to get everyone's name and city and state of birth correct. This way they will get a free swing at you having a low I.Q. and Alzheimer's. Your response will be? Laughter and agreement: "I think I am the worst one." (Take a one-down response when attacked.)

Introduction

Option 1: Leader says: "Now we are going to go around the room and everyone gets two minutes to say how they got here and how they feel about it. After that, the topic is closed from here on out."

Option 2: Leader says: "I know you all got here by mistake. The police are horrible these days on domestic violence calls, especially if you live in a city with a mandatory arrest policy. I know you guys were sleeping quietly in bed when your wife got drunk, slipped, fell down, bumped her head and called 911 and blamed you. You were cuffed and taken downtown."

The Wins, Slips and Miracles Game

PRETEND: Group leader says, *"We are all—myself included—going to pretend that we have an anger problem, although deep down inside, we know that we don't."*

SLIPS (in the first column) Group leader says, *"Now, I am going to write the word "SLIPS' in the first column. I want you to provide me with a list of all the ways anyone can express anger."* (Write down what they say. Turn to Chapter One in the workbook if anyone gets stuck. The list doesn't have to be complete; you can add more as you go along.)

If they say being quiet or clamming up for days is a slip, say: *"Well that is a little tricky. Actually, for those of us with an anger problem, that is progress. Besides, my goal is to keep you from being arrested again. I have never heard of anyone being arrested for sitting quietly on the couch and refusing to talk. For most of us, that is progress."*

WINS (in the second column): Group leader says, *"The next column is called, 'WINS.' Let's make a list of things people can do to show they are feeling good, happy or neutral.... Something other than expressing their anger, such as smile, give a compliment, leave quietly, agree, apologize, etc."* In order to have a win in this game, you must get angry, but not express it.

MIRACLES (in the third column): Group leader says, *"The third column is called, 'MIRACLES.' When you are in a situation where most people would get angry, and you don't... you don't even feel irritated... it's a miracle!"*

"Now, here is how it works. I will demonstrate. I will tell of a time in the last week when I got either a little irritated or a lot mad, and expressed it in some way, big or small. That would be a slip. Then I will give an example of a time I got angry and I did not express it. That would be a win."

Therapist: *Let's see. I got irritated at Joe for not giving his name, so I did some name-calling by saying his name was Runs-His-Mouth. That was a SLIP.*

A win? Let's see. When I turned into the parking lot, someone—probably one of you—thought I was taking too long and honked at me. I felt a flash of anger and had the impulse to put on the breaks and shoot them the finger, but instead I sped up a little bit and I did not make any rude gestures. That was a WIN. Okay, Joe... your turn.

Joe: *What am I supposed to do?*

Therapist: *Tell us about a time you have gotten angry and didn't express it.*

Joe: *Well, I was angry about coming here, because I really...*

Therapist: *That's good. Now, how did you express your anger?*

Joe: *I told my PO that it wasn't fair.*

Therapist: *Arguing with authority figures... I guess we need to add that to the slips column. Now... a time when you have been angry and not expressed it?*

Joe: *Well, my boss told me to do a bunch of stupid stuff, and I didn't say anything but, "Yes, sir!"*

Therapist: *You got it. Perfect example of a WIN.*

Continue around the room until everyone has participated and you have collected lots of examples of these behaviors. Then move on to introducing the workbook. Obviously, everyone will need his own copy.

WORKING THROUGH THE WORKBOOK

The Workbook gives you plenty of options and opportunities to keep the group busy for the prescribed number of sessions. They will be responsible for the material up through Chapter 3, including the Preface and the Introduction. The reading and the worksheets make excellent homework assignments, which they can bring back for discussion and evaluation by the group every week. And the Slips, Wins and Miracles routine works great as a warm-up to open each session.

Here are a few tips for keeping things moving:

- Don't hesitate to interrupt if someone is getting off track or missing the point. Simply say, "Wait a minute," make your point and keep moving.

- Anytime someone reports a slip, ask him to rewind the videotape, reset the scene, and ask, "What could you have done instead?"

- If you want a guy to expand on something say, "Tell me more about that."

- If a guy had a win or a miracle, give him a boost by saying, "How did you do that?"

- When someone reports a slip, always ask, "What could you do to make up for that?"

- Always encourage group feedback when a guy is talking through a slip or a make up issue.

Notes

Review Newton Hightower's Anger Busting 101: New ABCs for Angry Men and the Women Who Love Them (2002) for additional information listed below.

PREFACE

(p.16) Johari Window (From the work of Joe Luft and Harry Ingham). Best summarized in J. Luft Group Processes. Luft, J. (1970, 2nd Ed.) Group Processes: An Introduction to Group Dynamics. Palo Alto, CA: National Press Books.

INTRODUCTION

(p. 24) For more detailed description of the issues behind "Build-Up/Blow-Up" and "Expressive" theories of anger resolution, see Newton Hightower's *Anger Busting 101*, pgs 28-33.

(p. 27). The Anger Self-Assessment Test, taken from *Anger Busting 101*, pgs. 36-39

(p. 28) The revised STAXI-2, which is published by Psychological Assessment Resources, Inc. (PAR) contains 6 scales and 5 subscales for measuring different components of the experience, expression, and control of anger. Since the STAXI was first published in 1988, it has been widely used in research and has been translated and adapted in 10-12 languages and dialects.

CHAPTER 1

(p. 35) For more detailed discussion and additional examples of behaviors to stop, see *Anger Busting 101*, Chapter 1 (A = *Abstain from These Behaviors*), pgs. 43-68..

CHAPTER 2

(p. 73) For an interesting discussion of the role of beliefs in anger management, see *Anger Busting 101*, Chapter 2 (B = *Believe in these Principles for Peace, Happiness and Permanent Change*), pgs. 69-101.

CHAPTER 3

(pgs. 101-106) Deep and Shallow Doghouse communication strategies based on *Anger Busting 101*, Chapter 3 (C = *Communicate with These New Phrases*), pgs. 101-116.

(pgs 124-126) Example based on experience provided by Leon Hale, Houston Chronicle, July, 2002. Used by permission. © 2002 Houston Chronicle Publishing Company Division, Hearst Newspapers Partnership, L.P. All Rights Reserved.

CHAPTER 4

(pgs. 131-142) For a review of domestic violence statistics and the role of Pit Bull/ Cobra research in couples, see *Anger Busting 101,* Chapter 4 (*When to Get Rid of Your Man and Forget About Training*), pgs. 119-132.

CHAPTER 5

(pgs. 131-142) For more examples on drawing a line in the sand, see *Anger Busting 101,* Chapter 5 (*How to Get a Pit Bull's Attention and Make Him Behave*), pgs. 133-145.

CHAPTER 6

(pgs. 181-200) For more partner tactics, see *Anger Busting 101,* Section III Chapters 6-8 (*The New ABCs for Women Who Are Training Angry Men*), pgs. 147-172.

APPENDIX

(pgs. 201-208) For more information on Certification Training for Anger Resolution Therapy™, visit http://www.angerbusters.com.

For more information on Corporate Training in Anger Management, visit http://www.angermanagementseminar.com

Recommended Resources and References

The books and web sites listed below can provide further support and information to help you win your battle with anger.

Aronson, Harvey. (2004). *Buddhist Practice on Western Ground*. Boston, MA: Shambhala Publications.

Bradshaw, John. (1988). *Healing The Shame That Binds You*. Deerfield Beach, FL: Health Communications, Inc.

Bradshaw, John. (1992). *Creating Love: The Next Great Stage of Growth*. New York, NY: Bantam.

Clancy, Jo. (1996) *Anger and Addiction: Breaking the Relapse Cycle*. Guilford, CT: International Universities Press.

Ellis, Albert & Tafrate, Raymond. (1998). *How to Control Your Anger Before It Controls You*. New York, NY: Carol Publishing Group.

Eshelman, Elizabeth; Davis, Martha. & McKay, Matthew. (2000). Relaxation and Stress Reduction Workbook. Oakland, CA: New Harbinger Publications.

Gentry, W. Doyle. (1999). *Anger-Free: Ten Basic Steps to Managing Your Anger*. New York, NY: William Morrow.

Goleman, Daniel. (1995). *Emotional Intelligence*. New York, NY: Bantam Publishers.

Gottlieb, Miriam. (1998). *The Angry Self*. Phoenix, AZ: Zeig, Tucker and Thiesen.

Hightower, Newton. (2002). *Anger Busting 101: The New ABCs for Angry Men and the Women Who Love Them*. Houston: Bayou Publishing.

Hough, John. (1991). *Against the Wall*. New York, NY: Ballantine.

Justice, Blair & Justice, Rita. (1976). *The Abusing Family*. Norwell, MA: Kluwer Academic Publishers.

Luhn, Rebecca R. (1992). *Managing Anger: Methods for a Happier and Healthier Life*. Crisp Publications.

Maslin, Bonnie. (1994). *The Angry Marriage*. New York, NY: Hyperion.

McKay, Matthew & Rogers, Peter. (2000). *The Anger Control Workbook*. Oakland, CA: New Harbinger Publications, Inc.

Nuckols, Cardwell & Chickering, Bill. (1998). *Healing An Angry Heart: Finding Solace in a Hostile World*. Deerfield Beach, FL: Health Communications.

O'Hanlon, Bill. (1999). *Do One Thing Different: And Other Uncommonly Sensible Solutions to Life's Persistent Problems*. New York, NY: William Morrow.

Rosenstock, Harvey. (1988). *Journey Through Divorce*. New York, NY: Human Sciences Press.

Sonkin, Daniel & Durphy, Michael. (1982). *Learning to Live Without Violence: A Handbook for Men*. Volcano, CA: Volcano Press.

Sanders, Tim. (2002). *Love Is the Killer App: How To Win Business and Influence Friends*. New York, NY: Three Rivers Press.

Thurman, Chris. (1999). *The Lies We Believe*. Nashville, TN: Thomas Nelson.

Thurman, Chris. (1992). *The Truths We Must Believe*. Nashville, TN: Thomas Nelson.

Wexler, David. (1999). *Domestic Violence 2000*. New York, NY: W. W. Norton.

Online Resources

Angerbusters.com (2005). http://www.Angerbusters.com

Anger Management Seminars (2005). http://www.angermanagementseminar.com

Index

A

"anger seepage." *17*
ABCs *23*
    of anger *23*
    of working the workbook *42*
abstain
    from these behaviors *35–37, 45*
    the "A" in new ABCs *23, 180, 200*
accusing *181*
action *185*
addiction
    anger *41, 80, 197*
    pattern of *25*
    to rage *25*
Aikido *80*
Amazing Grace *93*
anger *23*
Anger Self Assessment Test *27*
announcing decision *164*
Assess
    the "A" in ABCs of the working the workbook *42, 105, 132*
Assess Your Doghouse Communication Skills *105*

B

"banned" behaviors *40, 42, 52.* See also behaviors to abstain from
"being right" *79*
"Build-up/Blow-up Theory of Anger." *24*
Banned Behavior Check List *43*
behaviors to abstain from
    banging walls *37*
    clucking *37*
    criticizing *38*
    cursing and profanity *36*
    interrupting *36*
    lecturing *38*
    mean tone of voice *37*
    mocking *37*
    name-calling *36*
    nonaffectionate touching *37*
    pointing *36*
    raising your voice *37*
    rolling eyes *37*
    sarcasm *37*
    sighing *37*
    slamming doors *37*
    speaking when angry *35*
    speeding *38*
    staring *35*
    staying *35*
    telling hero stories *37*
    threatening *36*
    throwing things *37*
    yelling *37*
belief system *185*
believe
    in these principles *73*
    the "B" in new ABCs *23, 73, 180, 200*
blame *23, 75*
blind spot *17, 18*
BREAK through
    the "B" of ABCs of working the workbook *42, 44*
bully *19*

C

"check-up from the neck up" *73*
Cannon, Walter *23*
careerism *81*
CBSSW phrases *102, 104*
Charting Your Progress Worksheet *66*
CHART Progress
    the "C" of ABCs of working the workbook *42, 66, 121*
Clements, Alan *76*
cobra *135, 139–141*
communicate *191*
    the "C" in new ABCs *23, 180, 200*
compulsion *25*
conditional semi-apology *104*
confronting *181*
consequences *163*
contracting for cooperation *166*

211

craving 26
criticism 23, 74

D

"De-Nial River" 15, 18, 19
Dead Sea 76
deep doghouse. *See doghouse*
denial 15, 26
doghouse 101
    deep 101, 102, 106, 108
    shallow 103, 114
    staying out of 101

E

Empire Strikes Back, The 80

F

"fight or flight" 23
family violence statistics 131

G

Golden Rule 76

H

habits 66
hero stories 37

I

Ingham, Harry 17
injustice 80
Instinct For Freedom 76
internal monologue 49
Involuntary Anger Management Group 200

J

Jedi master 80
Johari Window 17, 19

L

letter to God 119
love-saver 101
Love is the Killer App 80
Luft, Joe 17

M

marital tug-of-war 103
McGee, Robert 73
miracles 123, 125, 205
My Ideal Marriage Worksheet 141

O

obsession 26

P

Pasteur, Louis 93
phrases to avoid
    "but" 102
    "if" 104, 116
phrases to practice
    "I was stupid to have said that." 102
    "I was wrong." 103
    "What can I do to make it up to you"? 105
    "What can I do to make it up to you?" 104
    "You are right." 101, 108
Pit Bull 135–137, 155, 156
Pledge to Change Starting Right Now 29
pressure cooker 25, 35, 38, 45, 54
principles to believe in
    balancing life 81
    being compassionate 80
    being gracious 74
    being patient 76
    being wrong 79
    daily spritual meditation 83
    discipline 76
    empathy 75
    feeling awkward 81
    forgiveness 77
    humility 79
    losing 79
    practice kindness 74
    practice self-restraint 74
    self-exmination 75
    service 76
    surrendering 76
    understanding 80
psychological ping-pong 110

R

rageaholic 22, 25, 80, 101, 138, 155
reasoning 181
recovery driving 38, 76
rescue fantasies 26
Resignation Letter to God 75
resources for anger management 210
revenge 26, 74, 77
Rules of the Game 155

S

safety 158
Sanders, Tim 80
SARS 130
scapegoat 18
Scriptures
    Ephesians 4:15 74
    Ephesians 4:26-27 197
    Luke 11:4 77
Search For Significance, The 73
self-righteousness 79
self-stimulation 25
selfishness 75
shallow doghouse. *See doghouse*
shut up 25
Skywalker, Luke 80
slips 123, 125, 197, 205
Slips, Wins & Miracles Daily Anger Control Scorecard 126
Slips, Wins & Miracles Game 205
Solzhenitsyn, Alexander 76
spirituality 74
spiritual belief system 191
Spiritual Self-Assessment 84
Star Wars 80
STAXI-2 28

T

"Two Wolves" fable 198
teeter-totter effect 149
threatening 181
Time Allotment Inventory 81

U

unforgiveness 77
unpredictable behavior 26

V

victims of violence 132

W

"Why" questions 202
windowpane 17
winning 79, 102
wins 123, 125, 197, 205
withdrawal 26
Writing a New Script 54

About the Author

James A. (Jim) Baker is a longtime resident of Houston, Texas, where he has served the business world for many years as founder and chairman of Baker Communications. Baker Communications is one of America's leaders in the field of corporate training, serving the training needs of many of the nation's top companies, and being recognized for three consecutive years as an INC 500 company. Jim wrote and produced *Real Estate: Mastering the Negotiation Process*, a Nightingale Conant Corporation Audio Tape Series. He is also a Contributing Author to *The Sales Training Handbook: A Guide to Developing Sales Performance,* published by Prentice Hall and sponsored by the American Society for Training and Development. Jim is also a Certified Anger Resolution Therapist where he specializes in training other trainers in conflict resolution.

In addition to his professional accomplishments, Jim has been involved in the community over the years, assisting in projects and boards of directors such as:

- Board of Directors — *Jewish Institute for National Security Affairs*
- Board of Directors — *Greater Houston Partnership*
- Senior Consultant — *Dupont Corporation*
- Governor's Business Council

Founding Board Member — *Houston Drug Free Business Initiative*

Member — *Executive Committee of the Office for the Prevention of Developmental Disabilities* (appointed by the Governor of Texas)

Member — *Statewide Media Task Force on Dropout Prevention* (appointed by the Governor of Texas)

Board of Directors — *Corporation for Economic Development of Harris County, Inc.*

Board of Directors — *Cenikor*, Drug Rehabilitation Center

Member — *American Arbitration Association*

Board of Directors — *Houston Symphony*

Lifetime Member — *Houston Livestock Show and Rodeo*

Jim received his B.S. from the University of Rochester, a 30-hour Certificate in Behavioral Science from Rochester Institute of Technology, his M.S. from the State University of New York, and attended the South Texas College of Law. Jim is a co-founder of the National Center for Dispute Settlement of the American Arbitration Association, a past instructor for the Jesse H. Jones Graduate School of Business, Rice University and an Adjunct Professor for the University of Houston. He remains an active sponsor, author, and senior management and sales consultant.

Jim has two daughters, Bridget Baker Rogers and Sarah Baker McConnell.

Visit him online at http://www.angermanagementseminar.com.

Ordering Information

Additional copies of *The Anger Busting Workbook: Simple, Powerful Techniques for Managing Anger and Saving Relationships* are available at your favorite local or online bookstore, or directly from the publisher. Orders may be placed by phone, by mail, by FAX, or directly on the web. *Purchase orders from institutions are welcome.*

- ❑ *To order by mail:* Complete this order form and mail it (along with check, money order or credit card information) to Bayou Publishing, 2524 Nottingham, Houston, TX 77005-1412.

- ❑ *To order by phone:* Call (800) 340-2034

- ❑ *To order by FAX:* Fill out this order form (including credit card information) and fax to (713) 526-4342.

- ❑ *To place a secure online order:* Visit http://www.bayoupublishing.com

Name: _____

Address: _____

City: _____ ST: _____ Zip: _____

Ph: _____

FAX: _____

E-mail: _____

❑ Visa ❑ MasterCard ❑ American Express ❑ Discover

Charge Card #: _____

Expiration Date: _____

Signature: _____

Yes! Please send me _____ copies of *The Anger Busting Workbook* ($14.95 ea) _____

Sales Tax 6.25% (Texas Residents) _____

plus $4.00 postage and handling (per order) _____

Total $ _____

Bayou Publishing • 2524 Nottingham • Houston, TX 77005-1412 • Ph: (713) 526-4558
FAX: (713) 526-4342 • Orders: (800) 340-2034 • http://www.bayoupublishing.com